"BACH HAS A REMARKABLE GIFT . . . [HE] CONVINCE[S] AND CAPTIVATE[S] HIS LISTENERS."—*Time*

RICHARD BACH
NOTHING BY CHANCE

Is there a reason for every event that touches our lives? Richard Bach believed there was, and to find it, he set out on a great adventure. Here he tells about the magical summer when he turned time backward to become an old-fashioned barnstormer in an antique biplane . . . and let destiny be his copilot.

"BIOGRAPHY? FANTASY? METAPHYSICS? FICTION? NONFICTION? SELF-HELP? PHILOSOPHY? WITH BACH, THE POSSIBILITIES ARE INTENTIONALLY UNLIMITED."
—*The Salt Lake Tribune*

"JUST LOOK—HE IS UP THERE."
—Ray Bradbury

Books by Richard Bach

ONE
THE BRIDGE ACROSS FOREVER: A LOVE STORY
A GIFT OF WINGS
ILLUSIONS: THE ADVENTURES OF A RELUCTANT MESSIAH
BIPLANE
NOTHING BY CHANCE
STRANGER TO THE GROUND
JONATHAN LIVINGSTON SEAGULL
THERE'S NO SUCH PLACE AS FAR AWAY

NOTHING BY CHANCE

A Gypsy Pilot's Adventures in Modern America ❧

by Richard Bach

PHOTOGRAPHS BY PAUL E. HANSEN

An Eleanor Friede Book
A DELL BOOK

Published by
Dell Publishing
a division of
Bantam Doubleday Dell Publishing Group, Inc.
666 Fifth Avenue
New York, New York 10103

"If we are alert, with minds and eyes open, we will see meaning in the commonplace; we will see very real purposes in situations which we might otherwise shrug off and call 'chance'."

—from a lecture by Roland Bach

So this book is for Dad

Who has, kiting around in those rattletrap aeroplanes, a son that agrees.

NOTHING
BY CHANCE

CHAPTER ONE

THE RIVER WAS WINE beneath our wings—dark royal June Wisconsin wine. It poured deep purple from one side of the valley to the other, and back again. The highway leaped across it once, twice, twice more, a daring shuttlecock weaving a thread of hard concrete.

Along the thread, as we flew, came villages the color of new grass here in the end of spring, washing their trees in a clean wind. It was all the tapestry of summer beginning, and for us, of adventure.

Two thousand feet above the ground, the air was silver about us, sharp and cold, rising on up over our two old airplanes so deep that a stone dropped up into it would have been lost forever. Way high up in there I could just barely see the dark iron blue of space itself.

Both of these guys trusting me, I thought, and I don't have the faintest idea what's going to happen to us. It doesn't matter how many times I tell them, they still think since the whole thing is my idea I must know what I'm doing. I should have told them to stay home.

We swam the silver air like a pair of ocean minnows, Paul Hansen's sleek little sportplane darting ahead at a hundred miles an hour once in a while, then circling back to stay in sight of my fire-red, flower-yellow, slow-chugging open-cockpit wind-and-wire flying machine. Like giving the horses their rein, this turning our airplanes loose over the land and letting them fly back into their own time, with us hanging on for the ride and waiting to see the golden world of gypsy pilots forty years gone. We agreed on one thing—the grand old days of the barnstormer must still be around, somewhere.

Silent and trusting, Stuart Sandy MacPherson, age nineteen, peered over the edge of the cockpit in front of my own, looking down through his amber jumping-goggles to the bottom of an ocean of crystal air. Barnstormers always had parachute jumpers, didn't they? he had said, and parachute jumpers were always kids who worked their way and earned their keep selling tickets and putting up signs, weren't they? I had to admit that they were, and that I wasn't going to stand between him and his dream.

Once in a while now, looking down through the wind, he smiled to himself, ever so faintly.

We flew in a sheet of solid thunder. The clatter and roar of my Wright Whirlwind engine burst out just as loud and uncaring as it did in 1929, brand new, seven years before I was born, and it soaked us in the smell of exhaust fires and hot rocker-box grease; it shook us in the blast of propeller-torn air. Young Stu had once tried to shout a word across the space between our cockpits, but his voice was swept away in the wind and he hadn't tried again. Those gypsy pilots, we were learning, didn't do much talking when they flew.

The river turned sharply north, and left us. We pressed on overland into soft low meadowed hills, sun-glittering lakes, and farms everywhere.

Here it was . . . adventure again. The three of us and our two airplanes were the remnant of what had opened in spring as The Great American Flying Circus, Specialists in Death-

Defying Displays of Aerial Acrobatics, Authentic Great War Dogfighting, Thrilling and Dangerous Aeroplane Stunts, and the Incredible Free-Fall Parachute Leap. (Also, Safe Government-Licensed Pilots Take You Aloft to See Your Town From the Air. Three Dollars the Ride. Thousands of Flights Without a Mishap.)

But the other Great American aviators and airplanes had commitments in modern times; they had flown their planes back into the future from Prairie du Chien, Wisconsin, and had left Paul and Stu and I flying alone in 1929.

If we were to live in this time, we had to find grass fields and cowpastures to land in, close to town. We had to fly our own aerobatics, take our own chances, find our own paying passengers. We knew that five airplanes, a full circus, could bring out crowds of weekend customers; but would anyone move on a weekday to watch just two airplanes, and those unadvertised? Our fuel and oil, our food, our search for yesterday and our way of life depended upon it. We weren't ready to admit that adventure and the self-reliant individual had had their day.

We had thrown away our aeronautical charts, along with the time they came from, and now we were lost. There in the middle of the high cold silver roaring air, I thought we might be somewhere over Wisconsin or northern Illinois, but that was as far as I could pin it down. There was no north, no south, no east, no west. Only the wind from somewhere, and we scudded along before it, destination unknown, circling here over a town, over a meadow, over a lakeside, looking down. It was a strange afternoon without time, without distance, without direction. America spread from horizon to horizon before us, wide and big and free.

But at last, low on fuel, we circled a town with a little grass runway near at hand, and a gas pump and a hangar, and we got set to land. I had hoped for a hayfield, because old barnstormers always landed in hayfields, but the village sparkled with a certain magic lostness. RIO, it said, black letters on a silver water tower.

Rio was a hill of trees rising out of the low hills of earth, with rooftops down beneath the green and church spires like holy missiles poised pure white in the sun.

Main Street stretched two blocks long, then fell back into trees and houses and farmland.

A baseball game raged at the school field.

Hansen's trim Luscombe monoplane was already circling the airstrip, down to its last few gallons of gas. He waited for us, though, to make sure that we didn't change our mind and fly off somewhere else—for had we separated in that unknown land, we never would have seen each other again.

The strip was built on the edge of a sudden hill, and the first quarter of it lay at a fierce angle that must have made fine skiing, in winter.

I turned and landed, watching the green grass cartwheel up in slow motion to touch our wheels. We taxied to the deserted gas pump and shut down as Paul swished in overhead to land. His plane disappeared over the hillcrest as he touched down, but in a minute it reappeared, engine chugging softly, and rolled down the slope to us. With both engines silent at last, there was not a sound in the air.

"I thought you were never going to see this place," Paul said, unfolding from the Luscombe. "What took you so long? Some barnstormer you are. Why didn't you find a field two hours ago?"

He was a wide powerful man, a professional photographer, concerned because the world's image wasn't quite as beautiful as it should be. Under a carefully combed shock of black hair he had the look of a gangster trying hard to go straight.

"If it was me only, be no problem," I said, taking the bags that Stu handed down from the biplane. "But pickin' a place where your ground-hog airplane could fly from . . . yes sir, *that* was the problem."

"What do you think," Paul said, letting the slur about his airplane go by, "should we try a jump today, late as it is? If we want to eat, we'd better find some paying passengers."

"I don't know. Up to Stu. Up to you. You're supposed to be leader today."

"No, I'm not. You know I'm not the leader. You're the leader."

"OK, then. If I'm the leader, I say let's go up and do some aerobatics first and see what happens before we push poor Stu overboard."

"That means I have to unload my airplane."

"Yes, Paul, that means you have to unload your airplane."

As he turned to his task, a red pickup truck rolled from the highway and onto the dirt road leading to the airport gas pump. There were red letters on the side: AL'S SINCLAIR SERVICE. And according to the name stitched on his pocket, it was Al himself aboard.

"Quite some airplanes there," Al called, slamming the hollow steel door with a hollow steel slam.

"Sure are," I said. "Kind of old."

"I'll bet. You want some gas, I guess?"

"In a little while, maybe. Just flyin' through, barnstormin' a bit. Think it might be OK to try and hop a few passengers out of here? Folks see the town from the air?" A fifty-fifty chance. He could accept us or he could throw us off the field.

"Sure, it'd be OK! Glad to have you! Do a lot of good for the airport if we could get people to come out here, in fact. They've just about forgotten we *have* an airport, in town." Al looked over the leather rim into the old cockpit. "Barnstorming, you say. Rio's a big enough town for you?" He pronounced it Rye-O. "Population 776?"

"776 is just right," I said. "We'll go up for some aerobatics for a while, then come get gas. Stu, why don't you get the signs up now, out on the road?"

Without a word, the boy nodded, picked up the signs, (red letters on white linen, *FLY $3 FLY*) and strode silently off toward the highway, earning his keep.

The only way for a barnstormer to survive, we knew, is for him to fly passengers. Many passengers. And the only way to get passengers is first to attract their attention.

We had to make it quite clear that there was suddenly something strange and wild and wonderful going on at the airstrip, something that hadn't happened in forty years and might never happen again. If we could fire a spark of adventure within the hearts of townfolk we hadn't even seen, we could afford another tank of gasoline, and perhaps a hamburger.

Our engines burst alive again, bouncing hard echoes off the tin-hangar walls, flattening the grass back in two loud mechanical windstorms.

Helmets buckled, goggles down, throttles ahead to wide open power, the two old airplanes rolled, thumped, and lifted from green into deep clear blue, hunting passengers as hungrily as wolves hunt deer.

I looked down as we climbed over the edge of town, watching the crowd at the baseball game.

A couple of years ago, I wouldn't have cared. A couple of years ago my cockpit was all steel and glass and electronic controls and a sweptwing Air Force fighter that burned 500 gallons of fuel per hour, that could outrun sound. No need for passengers then, and if there were, three dollars wouldn't cover the cost of a flight, or a takeoff, or an engine start. It wouldn't even cover the Auxiliary Power Unit cost, to feed the electricity for the start. To use a fighter-bomber for barnstorming, we'd need two-mile concrete runways, a corps of mechanics and a sign to say, "FLY $12,000 FLY". But now, that three-dollar passenger was our entire livelihood; gas, oil, food, maintenance, salary. And at this moment we flew without any passengers at all.

At 3,000 feet over the cornfields we began our Death-Defying Display of Aerial Acrobatics. Paul's white wing snapped up, I had a quick rolling glance at the bottom of his airplane, streaked in oil and dust, and then he was diving right straight down. A second later the smooth-cowled nose pulled up again, and up, until his airplane was flying out toward the afternoon sun, roaring up past my biplane, then over on his back until he was upside-down, wheels in the sky, then nose back down again to finish the stunt. If he had a smoke flare on board, he would have traced a full vertical loop in the sky.

Way down in the crowd, I imagined I saw a face or two upturned. If we could fly just half the people watching that game, I thought, at three dollars each . . .

The biplane and I rolled into a great diving turn to the left, pushing down until the wind screamed in the wires. The black-green earth lay full in front of our nose, the wind pounded my leather helmet and set the goggles vibrating in front of my eyes. Then quickly back on the control stick and the ground fell away and blue sky filled the way ahead. Straight up, looking out at the wingtips, I saw the earth sweeping slowly around behind me, and I leaned my helmet back on the headrest and watched the fields and tiny houses and cars moving up from behind until they all stood directly overhead.

Houses, cars, the church spires, the sea of green leaves, all there in tiny full-color detail while I watched it above the biplane. The wind went quiet while we were upside-down and moving slowly through the air. Say we flew a hundred people. That would be three hundred dollars, or one hundred dollars for each of us. Less gas and oil, of course. But maybe we wouldn't fly that many. That would be one out of every eight people in town.

The world pivoted slowly to come back in front of the biplane's nose, and then beneath it again, with the wind screaming in the wires.

Across the air, Paul's airplane was standing still in the sky, its nose pointing straight up, his whole machine a blue-white plumb-bob on a long string down from heaven. Then, abruptly, it broke its string, pivoted left, and pointed down just as straightly.

It wasn't all quite as death-defying as our handbills had said; in fact, there's nothing an airplane can do to be death-defying, as long as it stays in its own place, the sky. The only bad times come when an airplane tangles with the ground.

From loop to roll to snap roll, the airplanes tumbled over the edge of town, gradually losing altitude, every minute a few hundred feet closer to that multicolored earth.

At last the monoplane came whistling toward me like some fast smooth rocket and we fell into the Authentic Great-War Aerial Dogfight, snarling around in rolls and hard-turning spirals and dives and zooms and slowflight and stalls. All the while, as we flew, a white smoke flare waited, tied to my left wing strut. We blurred the world about for a few minutes, juggling it all green and black and roaring wind from one hand to the other, the houses of the village now standing on this edge, now on that.

Say we made two hundred dollars clear, I thought. What would that be for each of us? What's three into two hundred? I slid under the monoplane, turned to the left, watched as Paul fell into place behind the biplane's tail. What the devil is three into two hundred? I watched him over my shoulder, rising and falling as he followed, turning hard to stay with the steep spiral of the biplane. Well, if it was $210, that would be $70 each. Seventy dollars each, not counting gas and oil. Say $60 each.

In that wild screaming hurricane of a power dive, I touched the button taped to my throttle. Thick white smoke burst from the left wing and I traced a death-spiral down to the airport, leveling just above the trees. As far as they could tell at the baseball game, that old two-winger had just been shot down in flames.

If it had worked with five planes, even for such a short while, it should work all summer with two. We don't really need the $60 each, all we really need is the gas and oil, and a dollar a day left for food. We can survive all summer if we just make that.

I slipped in to land as the smoke stopped, and rolled free down hill to the gas pump. One advantage of being shot down every time, I thought, is that you always get to the gas pump first.

Cold red fuel poured into the biplane's tank as Paul landed. He shut down his engine as he came down the hill, and coasted the last hundred feet with the propeller still and silver in front of him. Above the sound of the gasoline pouring from the nozzle under my glove, I could hear his tires crunching on the gravel that edged pump and office.

He waited for a moment in his cockpit, then slowly climbed out. "Boy, you sure take it out of me with all those turns. Don't turn so tight, will you? I don't have all that wing out there that you have."

"Only trying to make it look real, Paul. Wouldn't want to make it look too easy, would you? Any time you want, we can tie the flare to *your* airplane."

A bicycle turned in from the highway—two bicycles, going full speed. They slid to a stop that smashed grass into the rubber of their rear tires. The boys were eleven or twelve years old and after all that pell-mell arrival they didn't say a word. They just stood and stared at the airplanes, and at us, and back to the airplanes.

"Feel like flying?" Stu asked them, working his first day as Seller of Rides. With the five-plane circus, we had had a barker, complete with straw hat and bamboo cane and a roll of golden tickets. But that was behind us, and now it was up to Stu, who was more given to a quiet intellectual kind of persuasion.

"No, thanks," the boys said, and they were silent again, watching.

A car rolled onto the grass and stopped.

"Go get 'em, Stu-babe," I said, and made ready to start the biplane again.

By the time the Wright was chugging around, soft and gentle as a huge Model T engine, Stu was back with a young man and his woman, each laughing at the other for being so mad as to want a ride in this strange old flying machine.

Stu helped them up into the wide front cockpit, where he fastened them side-by-side under one seat belt. He called over the sound of the Model T for them to hold onto their sunglasses if they wanted to look out over the windscreen, and with that warning, stepped down and clear.

If they had fears about riding in this clattering old machine, it was too late now for mind-changing. Goggles down, throttle forward. The three of us were engulfed in the sound of a Model T gone wild, blasting hundred-mile winds back over us, sweeping the world into a grassy blur, jouncing at first, a sort of long muffled crash as the tall old wheels sped along the ground. Then the crash fell away with the earth and it was pure engine sound and wind beating us, and the trees and the houses shrank smaller and smaller.

In all that wind and engineblast and earth tilting and going small below us, I watched my Wisconsin lad and his girl, to see them change. Despite their laughter, they had been afraid of the airplane. Their only knowledge of flight came from newspaper headlines, a knowledge of collisions and crashes and fatalities. They had never read a single report of a little airplane taking off, flying through the air and landing again safely. They could only believe that this must be possible, in spite of all the newspapers, and on that belief they staked their three dollars and their lives. And now they smiled and shouted to each other, looking down, pointing.

Why should that be so pretty to see? Because fear is ugly and joy is beautiful, simple as that? Maybe so. Nothing so pretty as vanished fear.

The air smelled like a million grassblades crushed, and the sun lowered to turn it from silver air into gold. It was a pretty day and we were all three glad to be flying through the sky as if this were all some bright loud dream, yet detailed and clear as no dream had ever been.

Five minutes above the ground, turning into the second circle of town, my passengers were relaxed and at home in flight, unconscious of themselves, eyes bright as birds' for looking down. The girl touched her companion's shoulder, one time, to point out the church, and I was surprised to see that she wore a wedding ring. It couldn't have been too long ago that they had walked out the door of that church into a rice-storm, and now it was all a little toy place, a thousand feet below. That tiny place? Why, it had been so big then, with the flowers and the music. Maybe it was big only because it was a special time.

We circled down lower, took one last long look at the town, and slid in over the trees, air going soft in the struts and wires, to land. As soon as the tires touched, the dream was broken in the clatter and rumble of hard ground holding us as we moved, instead of soft air. Slower, slower and stopped at last where we began, the Model T ticking quietly to itself. Stu opened the little door and cast loose the seat belt.

"Thanks a lot," the young man said, "that was fun."

"That was *wonderful!*" his wife said, radiant, forgetting to adjust the mask of convention about her words and her eyes.

"Glad to fly with you," I said, my own mask firm in place, my own delight well down within myself and under tight control. There was so much more I wanted to say, to ask: Tell me how that all felt, first time . . . was the sky as blue, the air as golden for you as it is for me? Did you see that deep deep green of the meadow, like we were floating in emerald, there after takeoff? Thirty years, fifty years from now, will you remember? I honestly wanted to know.

But I nodded my head and smiled and said, "glad to fly with you," and that was the end of the story. They walked away arm in arm, still smiling, toward their car.

"That's it," Stu said, approaching my cockpit. "Nobody else wants to fly."

I came back from my far thoughts. "Nobody to fly? Stu, there's five cars out there! They can't all be just lookin'."

"They're going to fly tomorrow, they say."

If we had five airplanes, and more action going on, I thought, they'd be ready to fly today. With five airplanes, we'd look like a real circus. With two airplanes, maybe we're just a curiosity.

The old-timers, I thought, suddenly. How many of them ever survived, leading a gypsy-pilot's life?

CHAPTER TWO

IT WAS ALL SIMPLE AND free and a very good life. The barnstorming pilots, back in the twenties, just cranked their Jennies into the air and they flew to any little town and they landed. And then they took passengers up for joy-rides and they earned great bales of money. What free men, the barnstormers! What a pure life that must have been.

These same sky gypsies, full of years, had closed their eyes and told me of a sun fresh and cool and yellow like I had never seen, with grass so green it sparkled under the wheels; a sky blue and pure like skies never come, anymore, and clouds whiter than Christmas in the air. A land there was, in the old days, where a man could go in freedom, flying where he wanted to fly, and when; answering to no authority but his own.

I had asked questions and I had listened carefully to the old pilots, and way in the back of my mind I wondered if a man might be able to do the same thing today, out in the great calm Midwest America.

"On our own, kid," I heard. "Aw, it used to be great. Weekdays we'd sleep late, and work on the airplanes till supper-time, then we'd carry folks up to sunset and beyond.

Special times, pshaw, a thousand-dollar day was nothin'. Weekends we'd start flyin' at sunup and we wouldn't stop till midnight. Lines of people waitin' to fly, lines of 'em. Great life, kid. Used to get up in the morning . . . we'd sew a couple blankets together, sleep under the wing . . . get up and say, 'Freddie, where we goin' today?' And Freddie . . . he's dead now; a fine pilot, but he never came back from the war . . . and Freddie'd say, 'Where's the wind?'

" 'Comin' out of the west,' I'd say. 'Then we go east,' Freddie'd say, and we'd crank up the old Hisso Standard and throw in all our junk and off we'd go, headin' with the wind and savin' gas.

" 'Course the times got rough, after a while. There was the Crash in '29, and the folks didn't have much money to fly. We were down to fifty cents a ride where we had been five dollars and ten dollars. Couldn't even buy gas. Sometimes, two fellas workin', we'd drain gas out of one plane to keep the other flyin'. Then the Air-Mail came along and after that the airlines started up, needin' pilots. But for a while there, while it lasted, it was a good life. Oh, '21 to '29 . . . it was pretty good. First thing out, when you'd land, you'd get two boys out, and a dog. First thing, before anybody . . ." Eyes were closed again, remembering.

And I had wondered. Maybe those good old days aren't gone. Maybe they're still waiting now, out over the horizon. If I could find a few other pilots, a few other old planes. Maybe we could find those days, that clear clear air, that freedom. If I could prove that a man does have a choice, that he can choose his own world and his own time to live in, I could show that highspeed steel and blind computers and city riots are only one side of a picture of living . . . a side we don't have to choose unless we want to. I could prove that America isn't all really so changed and different, at heart. That beneath the surface of the headline, Americans are still a calm and brave and beautiful people.

When my vague little dream was known, a few folk of differing opinion rushed to stamp it to death. Time and again I heard that this was not just a chancy impractical quest, but impossible, without hope of success. The good old days are gone . . . why, everybody knows that! Oh, maybe it used to be a slow and friendly place, this country, but nowadays people will sue a stranger—and like as not a friend—at the drop of a hat. It's just the way people are, now. You go landing in a farmer's hayfield and he'll throw you in jail for trespassing, take your airplane for damages to his land and testify that you threatened the lives of his family when you flew over the barn.

People today, they said, demand the best in comfort and safety. You can't *pay* them to go up in a forty-year-old biplane all open-cockpit with wind and oil lashing back all over them . . . and you expect them to pay *you* for the pain of all that? There wouldn't be an insurance company—Lloyd's of London wouldn't cover a thing like that, for a cent less than a thousand dollars a week. Barnstorming, indeed! Keep your feet on the ground, friend, these are the 1960's!

"What do you think about a jump?" Stu asked, and snapped me back to afternoon Rio.

"Getting a bit late," I said, and the gypsy pilot and doom voices faded. "But, heck, a good calm day for it. Let's give it a try."

Stu was ready in a minute, tall and serious, shrugging into his main chute harness, snapping the reserve parachute across his chest, tossing his helmet into the front seat, making ready for his part of the quest. A bulky clumsy deep-sea diver, all buckles and nylon web over a bright yellow one-piece jumpsuit, he pulled himself into the forward cockpit and closed the little door.

"Allrighty," he said, "let's go."

I had a hard time believing that this lad, filled with inner fires, had chosen to study dentistry. Dentistry! Somehow we had to convince him that there was more to life than the makeshift security of a dentist's office.

In a moment, as we blasted off the ground and into the air, I was all of a sudden singing *Rio Rita*, making it *Rye-o Rita*. I knew only a part of the first line of the song, and it went over and over as we climbed to altitude.

Stu looked overboard with a strange faint smile, thinking about something way off in the distance.

Rita . . . Rye-o Ritah . . . noth . . . thing . . . sweetah . . . Rita . . . Oh-Rita. I had to imagine all the saxophones and cymbal-clashes over the thunder of the engine.

If I were Stu, I wouldn't be smiling. I'd be thinking about that ground down there, waiting for me.

At 2500 feet, we swung around into the wind, and flew directly above the airport. Rye-o Ritah . . . la . . . dee . . . deedah . . . deedah . . . oh Ritah . . . My-baby-an'-me-o, Ritah . . .

Stu came back from whatever far land it was he saw, and peered down over the side of his cockpit. Then, looking, he sat straight up and carefully dropped a bright roll of crepe paper overboard. It just missed the tail, unfurled into a long yellow-red-yellow streak of color and snaked straight down. I circled, climbing, and Stu was intent, watching the color. When it hit the ground, he nodded and smiled briefly back at me. We turned back on course for the airport, level at 4500 feet. I shuddered at the thought of actually jumping out of an airplane. It was a very long way down.

Stu opened his cockpit door while I slowed the biplane to ease the windblast for him. It was an odd feeling, to watch my front-seat passenger climb out onto the wing and make ready to get off while we were a mile in the air. He was going to go through with it, and I was afraid for him. There is a gigantic difference between standing on the ground talking glibly about parachute-jumping, and the fact itself, when one is standing on the wing, fighting the wind, looking down through empty empty air at the tiny little trees and houses and filaments of roads laid flat on the ground.

But Stu was all business now. He stood on the rubber mat of the wing root, facing the tail of the airplane, watching for his target to slide into view. He held onto a wing strut with one hand, the edge of my cockpit with the other. If anything, he was enjoying the moment.

Then he saw what he wanted to see; the center of the grass runway, and the windsock, barely visible in smallness. He leaned toward me. "GOIN' DOWN!" he said. And then, as simply as that, he vanished.

On the wing root, where he had been standing, was nothing. One instant there, talking, next instant gone. I wondered for a second whether he had ever been in the airplane at all.

I looked down over the side and saw him, a tiny figure, arms outstretched, falling straight down toward the ground. But it was more than falling. It was much faster than falling. He blurred down, fired from a cannon, right at the ground.

I waited for a long time as he changed from a tiny cross into a round speck. No parachute opened. It was not a good feeling, to wait for that chute. After an agonizing long while I knew that it was not going to open at all.

The very first jump of our two-plane circus and his parachute failed. I felt a little bit cold. His body might be that leaf-shaped dot there by the grove of trees that bordered the the airport, or the one by the hangars. Darn. We had lost our jumper.

I didn't feel sad for Stu; he knew what he was gambling

when he began parachute jumping. But just a second ago he had been standing right there on the wing, and now there was nothing.

His main chute must have failed and he didn't get the reserve open in time. I pulled back the throttle and spiraled down, watching the place where he had disappeared. I was surprised not be to shocked or remorseful. It was just a shame that it had happened this way, so early in the summer. So much for the dentistry.

In that instant, a parachute snapped open, way down below me. It came as quickly as Stu had gone from the wing, a sudden orange-white mushroom floating softly in the air, drifting very gently with the wind.

He was alive! Something had happened. At the last instant he finally wrenched the reserve chute into the wind, with one second left he had untangled from death, had pulled the ripcord, had lived. Any moment now he would be touching down with a wild terrible story to tell, and a word that he would never jump again.

But the fragile colored mushroom stayed long in the air, drifting.

We dived down toward it, the biplane and I, wires singing loud, and the closer we came to the parachute, the higher it was from the ground. We eased out of the dive at 1500 feet and circled a little man dangling by strings under a great pulsing dome of nylon.

He had altitude to spare. There never had been any trouble, there had never been any danger at all!

The figure swinging beneath the nylon waved across to me, and I rocked my wings in reply, grateful, puzzled that he should be alive.

And as we circled him, it wasn't we that turned, but his parachute, spinning around and around the horizon. A strange dizzy feeling.

The angle, of course! That's how he could be so high in the air now, when I was so sure he had hit the ground . . . the angle that I watched him from. I had been looking right down on top of him, and his only background was the wide earth all around. His death was an illusion.

He pulled one of the suspension lines and the canopy twisted swiftly around, one turn left, one turn right. He controlled the direction of the parachute at will; he was at home in his element.

It was hard to believe that this courageous parachute artist was the same softspoken boy that had shyly joined The Great American a week ago when it opened in Prairie du Chien. I thought of a maxim learned in twelve years' flying: Not what a man says, that matters, or how he says it, but what he does and how he does it.

On the ground, children popped like munchkins from the grass, and they converged on Stu's target.

I circled the chute until it was 200 feet above the ground, then held my altitude while the mushroom went on down. Stu swung his feet up and down a few times, last-minute calisthenics before his landing.

He was one moment drifting peacefully on the gentle air, and the next instant the ground rose up and hit him hard. He fell, rolled, and at once was on his feet again as the wide soft dome lost its perfect shape and flapped down around him, a great wounded monster of the air.

The monster-picture deflated with the parachute and became just a big colored rag on the ground, unmoving, and Stu was Stu in a yellow jump suit, waving OK. The children closed in on him.

When the biplane and I circled to land, I found that we had problems. The Whirlwind wasn't responding to its throttle. Throttle forward, nothing happened. A little farther forward and it cut back in with a sudden roar of power.

Throttle back and it roared on; full back, and it died away unnaturally. Something wrong with the throttle linkage, probably. Not a major problem, but there could be no passenger flying till it was fixed.

We came down rather unevenly to land, coasted over the hill and shut down the engine. Al, of AL'S SINCLAIR SERVICE, walked over.

"Hey, that was nice! There's quite a few folks here want to fly the two-winger. You can take 'em up this afternoon, can't you?"

"Don't think so," I said. "We like to end the day with the parachute jump . . . leave 'em with something nice to watch. We'll sure be here tomorrow, though, and love to have 'em come back."

What a strange thing to find myself saying. If that was our policy, I had just made it up. I would have been glad to fly passengers till sunset, but I couldn't do it with the throttle linkage as it was and it would not do to have them see that their airplane had to be repaired after every little flight around the airport.

Stu came in from the target, and the biplane captured quite a number of his young admirers. I stood near the airplane and tried to keep them from stepping through the fabric of the lower wings whenever they climbed up to look in the cockpits.

Most of the grown-ups stayed in their cars, watching, but a few came closer to look at the aircraft, to talk with Paul polishing the Luscombe, and with me, shepherding children.

"I was at the little league game when you guys flew over," a man said. "My boy was going crazy; he didn't know whether to look down at the game or up at the planes, so finally he sat on the roof of the car, where he could see both."

"Your jumper . . . he's a pretty young guy, isn't he?

Couldn't make me jump out of an airplane for all the money in the world."

"This all you do for a living, fly around places? You got a wife or anything?"

Of course we had wives, of course we had families just as involved in this adventure as we, but that wasn't something we thought people would want to hear. Barnstormers can only be carefree, footloose, fun-loving bright colorful people from another time. Who ever heard of a *married* sky gypsy? Who could imagine a barnstormer settled in a *house?* Our image demanded that we shrug the question aside and become the picture of gay and happy comrades, without a thought for the morrow. If we were to be shackled at all that summer, it would be by the image of freedom, and we tried desperately to live up to it.

So we answered with a question: "Wife? Can you imagine any woman let her husband go flyin' around the country in planes like these?" And we had lived a little more closely to our image.

Rio was changed by our arrival. Population 776, with a tenth of the town on the airport the evening after we arrived. And the biplane was grounded.

The sun was down, the crowd slowly disappeared into the dark and at last we were left alone with Al.

"You guys are the best thing that happened to this airport," he said quietly, looking toward his airplane in its hangar. He didn't have to speak loudly to be heard in the Wisconsin evening. "Lots of people think about us flying our Cessnas, they're not sure we're safe. Then they come out here and see you throw those airplanes around like crazymen and jump off the wings and all of a sudden they think we're *really* safe!"

"We're glad we can help you out," Paul said dryly.

The tree-frogs set in to chirping.

"If you want, you guys can stay in the office here. Give you a key. Not the best, maybe, but it beats sleepin' out in the rain, if it rains."

We agreed, and dragged our mountain of belongings in to carpet the office floor in a jagged layer of parachutes, boots, bedrolls, survival kits, ropes, and toolbags.

"Still don't see how we get all this stuff into the airplanes," Paul said, as he set down the last of his camera boxes.

"If you guys want a ride in town," Al said, "I'm goin' in; be glad to take you."

We accepted the offer at once, and when the airplanes were covered and tied, we leaped into the back of the Sinclair pickup truck. On the way, wind beating down over us, we divided up our income for the day. Two passengers at $3 each.

"It's kind of good," Stu said, "that all the airplanes from Prairie didn't stay. By the time you cut six dollars ten ways, there wouldn't be much left."

"They could have flown those other passengers, though," I said.

"I'm not worried," Paul offered. "I have a feeling that we're going to do pretty well, just by ourselves. And we made enough money for dinner tonight . . . that's all that matters."

The truck rolled to a stop at the Sinclair station, and Al pointed down the block to the A & W root-beer stand. "They're the last ones open and I think they close at ten. See you tomorrow out at the airport, OK?"

Al disappeared into his dark service station and we walked to the root-beer stand. I wished for once that I could turn off the barnstormer image, for we were watched as closely as slow-motion tennis balls by the drive-in customers of the Rio A & W.

"You're the fellows with the airplanes, aren't you?" The waitress who set our wooden picnic table was awed, and I wanted to tell her to forget it, to settle down and pretend that we were just customers. I ordered a bunch of hot dogs and root beer, following the lead of Paul and Stu.

"It's going to work," Paul said. "We could have carried twenty passengers tonight, if you weren't so afraid of working on your airplane for a few minutes. We could have done well. And we just got here! Five hours ago we didn't even know there *was* such a place as Rio, Wisconsin! We're going to make a fortune."

"Maybe so, Paul." As Leader for the day, I wasn't so sure.

Half an hour later we walked into the office and snapped on the light, blinding ourselves, destroying the night.

There were two couches in the office, which Paul and I claimed at once for our beds, pulling rank as the senior members of The Great American. We gave Stu the pillows from the couches.

"How many passengers are we going to carry tomorrow?" Stu asked, undisturbed by his low status. "Shall we have a little bet?"

Paul figured we would carry 86. Stu guessed 101. I laughed them both to scorn and said that the proper number was 54. We were all wrong, but at that moment, it didn't matter.

We snapped out the lights and went to sleep.

⚜ CHAPTER THREE ⚜

I WOKE UP HUMMING *Rio Rita* again; I couldn't get it out of my head.

"What's the song?" Stu asked.

"C'mon. You don't know *Rio Rita?*" I said.

"No. Never heard it."

"Ah . . . Paul? You ever stop to think that Stu, young Stu, probably doesn't know any songs from the war? What were you . . . born about . . . nineteen *forty-seven!* Good grief! Can you imagine anybody born in NINETEEN FORTY-SEVEN?"

"We're three caballeros . . ." Paul sang tentatively, looking at Stu.

". . . three gay caballeros . . ." I went on for him.

". . . three happy chappies, with snappy serappies . . ."

Stu was mystified at the odd song, and we were mystified that he wouldn't know it. One generation trying to communicate with another just half-way down, in that office-bunkhouse on a morning in Wisconsin, and getting nowhere, finding nothing but an uncomprehending smile from our parachute-jumper as he belted his white denim trousers.

We tried a whole variety of songs on him, and all with the

same effect. ". . . Shines the name . . . Rodger Young . . . fought and died for the men he marched among . . ."

"Don't you remember that song, Stu? My gosh where WERE you?" We didn't give him a chance to answer.

". . . Oh, they've got no time for glory in the infantry . . . oh, they've got no time for praises loudly sung . . ."

"What's next?" Paul was hazy on the lyrics, and I looked at him scornfully.

". . . BUT TO THE EVERLASTING GLORY OF THE INFANTRY . . ."

His face brightened. "SHINES THE NAME OF RODGER YOUNG! Shines the name . . . ta-ta-tata . . . Rodger Young . . ."

"Stu, what's the matter with you? Sing along, boy!"

We sang *Wing and a Prayer,* and *Praise the Lord and Pass the Ammunition,* just to make him miserable for not being born sooner. It didn't work. He looked happy.

We began the hike to town for breakfast.

"Can't get over that," Paul said at last.

"What."

"Stu's starting so young."

"Nothing wrong with that," I responded. "It's not when you start that makes your success in the world, but when you quit." Things come to you like that, barnstorming.

The card in the café window said *Welcome Travelers— Come In,* and above it was a neon sign with the paint gone from its tubes, and so saying EXIT.

It was a small place, and inside was a short counter and five booths. The waitress was named Mary Lou, and she was a girl from a distant and beautiful dream. The world went gray, she was so pretty, and I leaned on the table for support, before I sat down. The others were not affected.

"How's the French toast?" I remember saying.

"It's very good," she said. What a magnificent woman.

"Guarantee that? Hard to make a good French toast." What a beautiful girl.

"Guarantee. I make it myself. It's good toast."

"Sold. And two glasses of milk." She could only have been Miss America, briefly playing the part of waitress in a little Midwest village. I had been enchanted by the girl, and as Paul and Stu ordered breakfast, I fell to wondering why. Because she was so pretty, of course. That's enough right there. But that can't be—that's bad! From her, and from our crowded opening at Prairie du Chien, I was beginning to suspect that there might be tens of thousands of magnificent beautiful women in the small towns across the country, and what was I going to do about it? Be entranced by them all? Give myself up to bewitchment by ten thousand different women?

The bad thing about barnstorming, I thought, is that one sees only the swift surface, the sparkle in the dark eye, the brief glorious smile. Whether it's all emptiness or an utterly alien mind behind those eyes and that smile, is something that takes time to discover, and without the time, one gives the benefit of the doubt to the being inside.

Mary Lou was a symbol, then. Without knowing it, knowing only that one of the men at Table Four has ordered French toast and two milks, she has become a siren upon a murderous shore. And the barnstormer, to survive, must lash himself to his machine and force himself to be spectator only as he drifts by.

I went all through breakfast in silence.

There is Wisconsin so deeply in her words, I thought, it's almost Scottish. "Toast" was *toahst*, "two" was a gentle *too*, and my compadres' hashbrowns were *poataytoahs*. Wisconsin is Scottish-Swedish American with long long vowels, and

Mary Lou, speaking that language as her native tongue, was as beautiful to listen to as she was to look upon.

"I think it's about time for me to wash some clothes," Paul said over his coffee.

I was shocked from my girl-thoughts.

"Paul! The Barnstormer's Code! It breaks the Code to get all washed clean. A barnstormer is a greasy oily guy . . . you ever heard of a *clean* barnstormer? Man! What you tryin' to do?"

"Look. I don't know about you, but I'm going down to the Laundromat . . ."

"THE LAUNDROMAT! What are you, man, a big-city photographer or somethin'? We can at least go down to the river and beat our clothes out on some flat rocks! Laundromat!"

But I couldn't move him from the heresy and he talked about it with Mary Lou as we left.

". . . and on the drier, it works better on Medium than Hot," she said in her language and with a dazzling smile. "It doesn't shrink your cloathes. As much."

"The Great American Flying Laundry," Stu said to himself as he pushed our clothes into the machine.

While they thrashed around, we sauntered lazily through the market. Stu paused reflectively by the frozen-food locker at the rear of the wooden-pillared room.

"If we took a TV dinner," he mused, "and wired it on the back of the exhaust manifold, and ran the engine up for fifteen minutes . . ."

"There would be gravy all over the engine," Paul said.

We walked the blocks of Main Street under the wide leaves and deep shadow of daytime Rio. The Methodist church, white and lapstrake, pushed its antique needle-spire up out of sight in the foliage to anchor the building in the sky. It was a quiet day, and calm, and the only thing that moved was an occasional high branch to shift some dark shadow across the lawn. Here, a house with window-halves of stained glass. There, one with an oval-glass door all rose and strawberry. Now and then a window framed a fringed cut-glass lamp. Man, I thought, there is no such thing as time. This is no dusty jerking Movietone, but here and now, slow and soft and full fragrant color softly swirling down the streets of Rio, Wisconsin, United States of America.

Another church, as we walked, and here children were tended on the lawn, singing. Singing in earnest, *London Bridge is Falling Down*. And holding hands and making the bridge and ducking under. All there on the lawn, not giving us a glance, as though we were people traveled back from another century and they could see right through us.

Those children had been playing London Bridge forever on that lawn, and would go on playing it forever. We were no more visible to them than air. One of the women tending the game looked up nervously, as a deer looks up, not quite scenting danger, not quite ready to disappear into the forest. She didn't see us stopped and watching except in a sixth-sense way; no word was said, and London Bridge fell and claimed two more children, who in turn became another Bridge. The song went on and on, and we finally walked away.

At the airport, our airplanes waited just as we had left them. While Paul neatly folded his clothes in his very neat way, I stuffed mine into a bag and walked out to fix the throttle linkage on the biplane. It took less than five minutes of silent work in the slow quiet daytime hours that are a barnstormer's weekday.

Paul, who had been a sky-diver himself, once, helped Stu lay his main parachute canopy in the calm air of the hangar. By the time I wandered over to them, they were kneeling at the end of the long loom of nylon, deep in thought. Nobody moved. They just sat and thought, and paid me no mind.

"I'll bet you got problems," I said.

"Inversion," Paul said absently.

"Oh. What's an inversion?"

Paul just looked at the nylon lines and thought.

"I let the canopy come down on top of me yesterday," Stu said at last, "and when I got out from under I got the suspension lines mixed a little."

"Ah." I could see it. The smooth bundle of cords that ran from Stu's harness to the edge of the canopy was marred by one pair, twisted.

"OK. Unhook your Capewell there," Paul said suddenly, "and run it right through here." He spread a set of cords apart hopefully.

Stu clicked the harness quick-release and did as Paul asked, but the lines were still twisted. It fell quiet again in the hangar, and the quiet was weighted down at the corners with very heavy thinking.

I couldn't stand the atmosphere, and left. It was as good a time as any to grease the Whirlwind's rocker boxes. Outside, there was no sound but sun and growing grass.

Around noontime, engine greased and parachute untangled, we walked the familiar road to the EWT Café, sat down in booth Four for lunch and were charmed again by the enchantress Mary Lou.

"You get used to it all pretty quickly; you get known, don't you?" Paul said, over his roast beef. "We've been here a day and we know Mary Lou and Al and most everybody knows who we are. I can see where we could feel pretty secure, and not want to go on."

He was right; security is a net of knowns. We knew our way around town, we knew the main industry was the glove factory which shut down for the day at 4:30 and released potential customers for us.

We were safe here, and the fear of the unknown beyond

Rio had begun to creep in upon us. It was a strange feeling, to begin to know this little town. I felt it, and rather moodily tasted my chocolate milkshake.

It had been the same way at Prairie du Chien, a week ago, when we opened. We were secure there, too, with $300 guaranteed just to appear for the Historical Days weekend, plus all the money we could make carrying passengers.

In fact, by Saturday afternoon, in great crowds of people emerging from winter, we had earned nearly $650. There was no denying it was a good start.

Part of the guarantee, though, was the Daring Display of Low-Altitude Stunt Flying, and in an hour quieter than the others, I thought I might as well run my Handkerchief Pickup.

Snagging the white square of silk from the ground with a steel hook on my lower left wingtip wasn't all that difficult, but it looked very daring and so made a good air-circus stunt.

The biplane had climbed like a shot into the wind, which had freshened to a brisk 20 miles per hour. The stunt felt right, in all the noise and engine-thunder, the wing was coming down at just the right instant; but each time I looked out to see an empty hook, and back over my shoulder I could see the handkerchief untouched on the grass.

By the third try, I was annoyed at my bumbling, and concentrated wholly on the task, tracking the white silken spot directly down the line it should go, seeing nothing else but the green blur of ground a few feet below, moving 100 miles per hour. Then a full second ahead of time, I tilted the wing down, waited until the white had blurred into the hook and pulled up in what was planned to be a victorious climb.

But I had missed it again. I sat tall in the seat and looked out at the wingtip, to make sure that the hook was still there. It was, and it was empty.

Those people waiting on the ground must think this is a

poor kind of flying circus, I thought grimly, that can't even pick up a plain old handkerchief in three tries.

The next time I turned hard down in a steep diving pass and leveled off just at the grasstops, a long way from that mocking handkerchief, and on a line directly into it. I will get it this time, I thought, if I have to take it ground and all. I glanced at the airspeed dial, which showed 110 miles per hour, and eased a tiny bit forward on the control stick. The grass flicked harsh beneath the big tires, and bits of wild wheat spattered against them. A tiny turn left, and just a little lower.

At that instant, the wheels hit the ground, and they hit it hard enough to jerk my head down and blur my sight. The biplane bounced high into the air and I eased forward again on the stick and made ready to drop the wing for the pickup.

Then in that second there was a great snapping explosion, the world went black and the engine wailed up in a shriek of metal running wild.

The prop is hitting the ground I am crashing what happened the wheels must have torn off I have no wheels and now the propeller is hitting the ground hitting dirt we're going over on our back way too fast dirt flying pull up pull up full power flying again but nothing I'm getting nothing out of the engine prop's gone where land wires trees field wind . . . All at once that concussion of thought burst across me. And behind it, the dead knowing that I had crashed.

✄ CHAPTER FOUR ✄

I FELT THE TREMENDOUS POWER of the airplane smashing into the ground, clenched down tight in the cockpit, jammed full throttle and jerked the machine back into the air. The only thing I got from the throttle was a loud noise forward. There was no power at all. The biplane staggered back up on sheer momentum.

We were not going to make it over the telephone wires ahead. It was strange. They had been close, at 110 mph, but now they were not close. We turned into the wind by reflex, and at full throttle, engine screaming a hundred feet in the air, everything slowed down. I felt the airplane trembling on a stall and I was keen and aware of it, knowing that to slow any more would be to pitch nose-down into the ground. But I knew the biplane, and I knew that we would just hang there and come down slowly slowly into the wind. I wondered if the people on the ground were frightened, since it must all look pretty bad; a big burst of dirt and wheels flying off and the strange howling of the engine and the shuddering high in the air before it falls. Yet the only fear I felt was their fear, of how this all must look from the ground.

We came down in slow motion, facing the wind, into the

tall grass. Not a single obstacle to clear. The earth came leisurely up to meet us and at last it brushed us lightly with its green. In that moment the engine was of no further use, and I flicked the magneto switch off. We slid slowly through the weeds, less than 20 miles per hour, and with nothing else to do, I moved the mixture lever to Idle-Cutoff and the fuel selector to Off. There was no shock of touchdown, no lurching forward in the seat. All in very slow motion.

I was impatient to get out and see what had happened, and had my safety belt off and was standing up in the cockpit before we had slid to a stop.

The biplane tilted wildly down, right wing low, grass and dust settling through the air. My beautiful darn airplane.

It did not look good. The right lower wing was a mass of wrinkles, which could only mean a broken spar beneath the fabric. How sad, I thought, standing there in the cockpit, to end this barnstorming all so quickly after it had started.

I watched myself very carefully, to see when I would begin to be afraid. After this sort of thing happens, one is supposed to be afraid. The fear was taking its time, though, and more than anything, I was disappointed. There would be work ahead, and I would much rather fly than work.

I stepped out of the airplane, all alone in the field before the crowd arrived, pushed my goggles up and looked at the machine. It was not easy to be optimistic.

Besides the spar, the propeller was bent. Both blades, bent hard back from the tips. The right landing gear had broken loose, but not off, and had smashed back into the wing when we landed. That was the extent of the damage. It was not nearly so bad as it had felt.

Off across the field, the men walking, the boys running, the crowd came to see what was left of the old airplane. Well, I thought, I guess it had to be, guess I'd want to come over and look, if I were in their place. But what had happened was now old news to me, and the thought of saying it over and over again was not one that I relished. Since my fear still hadn't arrived, I would spend the time thinking of some good understatements to fit the occasion.

A big official truck rolled out across the grass. GO NAVY, it said in big white letters, and on top of it was mounted a pair of loudspeakers to reinforce the words. At this point going Navy was a much sounder bet than going Air Force.

Paul Hansen had been first to arrive, cameras around his neck, out of breath.

"Man . . . I thought . . . you . . . had bought it . . ."

"What do you mean?" I said. "We just touched down a little hard there. Felt like we ran into something."

"You don't . . . know. You hit the ground, and then . . . went way over . . . on your nose. I thought you . . . going to nose over for sure . . . on your back. It was a bad . . . scene. I really thought . . . you had it."

He should have had his breath back by now. Was the sight of the crash so bad that it could affect him so? If anybody had a right to be concerned, it was me, because it was my airplane all bent up there in the grass.

"Oh, no, Paul. Not a chance of going over. Did it really look that way?"

"Yeah. I thought . . . my God . . . Dick's bought it!"

I didn't believe him. It couldn't have been that bad. But thinking back, I remembered that the first impact had been very hard, though, and the sound of that explosion. And we did nose forward then, too. But nothing like we were going over.

"Well," I said, after a minute, "You got to admit that's a pretty hard act to follow." I felt springs loosening inside me, springs that had been tight in the air, to let me feel every tiny motion of the airplane. Now they were loosening, and I felt relaxed, except that I didn't know how long it would take to fix the airplane. That was the only tense thought. I wanted to fix the plane as soon as possible.

Thirty hours later, the biplane had been repaired, tested and was flying passengers again.

It is kind of a miracle, I thought, and I wondered at it.

When we left Prairie du Chien, Rio was the Unknown. And now, with Rio become Known, we felt the tug of security, and were uneasy.

The wind came up that afternoon and it changed Stu MacPherson at once from parachute jumper to a groundling ticket-seller.

"It's about fifteen miles an hour now," he said, worried. "That's a bit too much for me to feel good about jumping."

"Aw, c'mon," I said, wondering how powerful a wind could be on the big silken dome. "Fifteen crummy miles an hour? That can't hurt you." It would be fun to know, too, whether Stu could be bullied out of his better judgment.

"That's getting pretty windy. I'd rather not jump."

"We got all these people coming out to see you. Crowd's gonna be unhappy. Somebody said yesterday that your jump was the first ever made on this field. Now everybody's all set to see the second. You better jump." If he gave in, I had a lecture all prepared on how only weaklings give in to what they know isn't right.

"Fifteen miles is a lot of wind, Dick," Paul said from the hangar. "Tell you what. We have to test the canopy out, make sure that the inversion's gone. Why don't you strap on the harness for us and we'll throw the canopy up into the wind and see that it opens out all right."

"I'll strap on your parachute," I said. "I'm not afraid of your parachute."

Paul brought the harness over and helped me strap into it, and as he did, I remembered the stories I had heard in the

Air Force of pilots dragged about helplessly by parachutes in the wind. I began, in short, to have second thoughts.

But by that time I was strapped in, my back to the wind, which seemed to be blowing much harder now, and Paul and Stu were down by the canopy laid on the grass, ready to throw it up into the quick-moving air.

"Ready to go?" Paul shouted.

"Just a minute!" I didn't like his word about "going," for I meant to stay right where I was. I dug my heels into the ground, unsnapped the safety catch on the quick release that would spill the canopy if anything went wrong.

"Don't punch the Capewell," Paul said. "It will get the canopy all tangled up again. If you want to spill the chute, pull on the bottom risers. You ready?"

Directly downwind was a low fence of timbers and steel cables. If I dragged, I'd drag right into it. But then again I'm 200 pounds all dug in here, and no little breeze could drag that much all the way to the fence. "Ready!"

I braced against the wind and Paul and Stu tossed the skirt of the canopy into the air, with what seemed like altogether too much enthusiasm. The wind caught the chute at once, it popped out like a racingboat spinnaker, and every ounce of that force snapped down the risers and into my shoulders. It was like a tractor lurching into gear, and all hooked to me.

"HEY!" I flew out of my special braced place, and out of the second place I dug my boots into, and out of the third. I thought of losing my balance behind this big thing, and being whipped across that fence. The monster jellyfish pulled me in jerks, wham-wham-wham across the ground while Paul and Stu just stood and laughed. It was the first time I had heard Stu laugh.

"Hold on there, boy!"

"This is just a little breeze! This is nothing! Hey, hang on!"

I got the idea about wind and parachutes and grabbed for

the lower risers to collapse the thing while I skidded for the fence. I pulled, but nothing happened. If anything, I skidded faster, and nearly lost my balance.

At that point I ceased to care about the delicacy of Stu's canopy, and pulled hard on all the bottom lines I could get hold of. Very suddenly the chute collapsed and I was standing in the mild wind of afternoon.

"What's the matter?" Paul called. "Couldn't you hold the thing?"

"Well, I thought I'd just as soon not cut your lines all up on the fence, there. Save you some repair work."

I unsnapped the harness, quickly. "Stu, I don't think you'd better jump today. This wind's up a little too high. Of course you want to jump anyway, but it's wiser for you just to stay down this afternoon. I think it's a lot wiser."

We rounded up the giant canopy and bundled it into the calm of the hangar.

"You really ought to jump sometime, Richard," Paul said. "There's nothing like it. That's real flying. Man, you get up there, no engine or nothing. Just . . . you. Dig? You really ought to do it."

I have never had any intention of jumping out of an airplane and Paul's pitch did not make me eager to start now.

"Sometime," I said. "I'll give it a whirl, when the wings fall off my airplane. I want to start right out with a free-fall, and not go through all those static-line things they make you do in the jump schools. At the moment, let us say that I'm not quite ready to begin my jumping career."

Al's Sinclair pickup truck arrived, and with him in the cab was a tall distinguished fellow we met as Lauren Gilbert, who owned the airport. Lauren couldn't do enough to make us welcome. He had learned to fly when he was fifty years old, was completely caught up in the fun of flying, and had just yesterday passed the tests to earn his instrument-flight license.

Our policy insisted that he have a free ride, since he owned the field, and the biplane was airborne ten minutes later on its first flight of the afternoon. This was our advertising flight; the first one up, to tell the town that we were in business and already flying happy passengers and why weren't they up in the sky with us, looking down at the city?

We had to work a flight pattern over each town, and the pattern over Rio was takeoff west, climb south and east in a shallow left turn, level at 1,000 feet, turn back and circle the town in a right turn all the way to the airstrip, steep turns north, slip down over the telephone wires, land. This came to a twelve-minute ride, gave our passengers a view of their home, the feeling of the freedom of flying, and an adventure to talk about and paste into scrapbooks.

"That's pretty nice," Lauren said as Stu opened the door for him. "You know that's the first time I've ever been up in an open-cockpit airplane? That's really flying. That's wonderful. The wind, you know, and that big old engine up there . . ."

A pair of boys appeared, Holly and Blackie by name, wheeling their bicycles, and we all walked together to the office after Lauren's ride.

"Boys, you want to go for a ride?" he asked down at them.

"We don't have any money," Holly said. He was perhaps thirteen years old, of bright and inquisitive eye.

"Tell you what. You come out here and wash down my Cessna, polish it all up, and I'll pay for your rides. How's that sound?"

There was an uncomfortable silence from the boys.

"Ah . . . no thanks, Mister Gilbert."

"What do you mean? Boys, this is probably the last of these old biplanes you'll ever see! You'll be able to say that you've flown in a biplane! And there's not many people left, even grown-ups, anymore, that can say that they've flown in a real biplane."

Silence again, and I was surprised. I would have worked on that Cessna for a year, when I was thirteen, to get a ride in an airplane. Any airplane.

"Blackie, how about you? You help get my airplane all clean and there's a ride for you in the old biplane."

"No . . . thanks . . ."

Lauren was selling them hard. I was astonished at their fears. But the boys looked down at the floor and said nothing

At last, very reluctantly, Holly agreed to the deal, and all of Lauren's firepower turned on Blackie.

"Blackie, why don't you go on up with Holly, you boys can fly together."

"I don't think so . . ."

"What? Why, if little Holly here flies and you don't, you're a sissy!"

"Yeah," Blackie said quietly. "But it doesn't matter, 'cause I'm bigger than him."

At last, however, all resistance fell to Lauren's enthusiasm and the boys climbed aboard the biplane, expecting the worst. The engine burst into life, fanning their sober faces with exhaust wind; a moment later we were lifting up into the sky. A thousand feet higher, they were peering down over the leather edge of the front cockpit, pointing down once in a while and occasionally shouting to one another above the noise. By the end of the flight, they were veterans of the air, laughing through the steep turns, looking fearlessly straight down the wing to the ground.

When they stepped down out of the cockpit, back safely on the earth, they maintained a dignified calm.

"That was fine, Mr. Gilbert. It was fun. We'll come work this Saturday, if you want."

It was hard to tell. Would they remember the flight? Would it ever be a meaningful thing to them? I'll have to come back in twenty years, I thought, and ask if they remember.

The first of the automobiles arrived, but they arrived to watch, not to fly.

"When's the parachute jump?" The man got out of his car to ask. "Pretty soon now?"

"It's too windy today," Stu told him. "I don't think we're going to do the jump today."

"What do you mean? I came all the way out here to see the parachute jump and here I am and you say it's too windy. Look, the wind isn't hardly blowing at all! What's the matter? You scared to jump, you going to chicken out?"

His voice had just enough fire to burn.

"Boy, I am glad you came out!" I turned on him in genuine heartiness, protecting young MacPherson. "Am I glad to see you! Gee, we were afraid that we'd have to scrub the jump today because the wind, but heck, here you are. Wonderful! You can make the jump for Stu, here. I always thought the boy was a little chicken anyway, aren't you, Stu?" The more I talked, the more annoyed I got with the guy. "Hey, Paul! We got a jumper! Bring the chute over and we'll get him all suited up!"

"Well, just a minute . . ." the man said.

"Do you want to go out at three thousand, or four? Whatever you say is OK with us. Stu's been using the windsock for a target, but if you want to come in a little closer to the wires . . ."

"Hey, friend, I'm sorry. I didn't mean that I . . ."

"No, that's fine. We're really glad to find you. We wouldn't have had the jump at all today without you. We sure appreciate your coming up and making it for us . . ."

Paul caught the idea and hurried our way, carrying Stu's parachute and helmet.

"I don't think I better. I understand about the wind," the man said, and waved and walked quickly to his car. The whole scene could have been from a screenplay, it worked so well, and I put the method down on my list to use again with unhappy jump-expecters.

"What would you have done if he didn't back out?" Stu said. "What if he said he wanted to jump?"

"I woulda said fine, and popped him into that chute like nothin' flat. I was darn ready to take him up and throw him over the side."

For a while the people sat in their cars and watched, and wouldn't budge when Stu walked to their windows.

"Come on up and fly!" he said at one window. "Rio from the air!"

The figure inside shook its head. "I like to see it from the ground."

If this was typical modern barnstorming, I thought, we were dead; the good old days were truly gone.

At last, about 5:30 in the afternoon, a fearless old farmer drove in. "I got a place about two miles down the road. Fly me over and see it?"

"Sure thing," I said.

"What'll it cost me?"

"Three dollars cash, American money."

"Well, what are we waitin' for, young fella?"

He couldn't have been less than seventy, but he lived the flight. Snowy hair streaming back in the wind, he pointed the way to fly, and then down to his house and barn. It was as neat and pretty as a Wisconsin travel poster; bright green grass, bright white house, bright red barn, bright yellow hay in the loft. We circled twice, to bring a woman out on the grass, waving. He waved back wildly to her and kept waving as we flew away.

"A good ride, young fella," he said when Stu guided him

down from the cockpit. "Best three dollars I ever spent. First time I been up in one of these machines. Now you made me sorry I didn't do it a long time ago."

That ride started our day, and from then till sunset I stayed in the cockpit, waiting only long enough on the ground for new riders to step aboard.

Stu caught on to a nice bit of passenger psychology, and took to saying, "How'd you like it?" when the flyers deplaned. Their clear fun and wild enthusiasm convinced the doubtful waiting to go ahead and invest in flight.

A few passengers came back near my cockpit after their flight and asked where they might learn to fly, and how much it might cost. Al and Lauren had been right, thinking we could do something for Rio aviation. One more airplane hangared at the airstrip would increase the flying by 25 percent, three more airplanes would double it. But the nature of the barnstormer is to come and be gone again all in a day, and we never heard what happened at Rio after we flew away.

The sun dropped down around us. Paul and I went up for one last formation flight for fun and watched the lights slowly sparkle on, down in the dark streets. When we landed, we could hardly see to taxi, and we felt as if we had been working much longer than one afternoon.

We covered the airplanes, paid the gas bill and just as we were all cocooned in our sleeping bags, and as Stu had un-cocooned at the request of his seniors to turn out the light, I saw a pair of beady black eyes watching me from under the toolkit, near the door.

"Hey, you guys," I said. "We got a mouse in here."

"Where do you see a mouse?" Paul said.

"Tool-kit. Underneath it."

"Kill him. Get him with your boot, Stu."

"PAUL, YOU BLOODTHIRSTY MURDERER!" I

shouted. "There will be no killing in this house! Pick up that boot and you got that mouse and me both to face, Stu."

"Well, sweep him out, then," Paul said, "if you're going to be that way."

"No!" I said. "The little guy deserves a roof over his head. How would you like somebody to sweep you out in the cold?"

"It's not cold outside," Paul said peevishly.

"Well, the principle of the thing. He was here before we came. This is his place more than ours."

"All right, all right," he said. "Leave the mouse there! Let the mouse walk all over us. But if he steps on me, I'm gonna pound him!"

Stu obediently snapped out the lights and groped back to his couch-pillows on the floor.

We talked in the dark for a while about how kind our hosts had been, and the whole town, for that matter.

"But you notice we carried no women here, or almost none?" Paul said. "There was hardly one female passenger. We had all kinds of them at Prairie."

"We made all kinds of money, and we didn't quite do that here," I said.

"How'd we do in all, by the way, Stu?"

He reeled off statistics, "Seventeen passengers. Fifty-one dollars. " 'Course we spent nineteen for gas. That's what..." he paused for figuring, ". . . ten bucks each, today, about."

"Not bad," Paul said. "Ten bucks for three hours' work. On a weekday. That works out to fifty dollars a week with all expenses paid except food, and not counting Saturday and Sunday. Hey! A guy can make a living at this!"

I wanted very much to believe him.

⚜ CHAPTER FIVE ⚜

FIRST THING NEXT MORNING, Paul Hansen was on fire. He was all crushed up in his sleeping bag, and from the end of it, from just by his hatbrim, a veil of smoke curled up.

"PAUL! YOU'RE ON FIRE!"

He didn't move. After a short aggravated pause, he said, "I am smoking a cigarette."

"First thing in the morning? Before you even get up? Man, I thought you were on fire!"

"Look," he said. "Don't bug me about my cigarettes."

"Sorry."

I surveyed the room, and from my low position it looked more like some neglected trash-bin than ever. In the center of the room was a cast-iron wood-burning stove. It said *Warm Morning* on it, in raised iron, and its draft holes looked at me with slitted eyes. The stove did not make me feel very welcome.

Lapping all around its iron feet were our supplies and equipment. On the one table were several old aviation magazines, a tool-company calendar with some very old Peter Gowland girl-shots, Stu's reserve parachute, with its altimeter and stopwatch strapped on. Directly beneath was my red plastic clothes bag, zippered shut, with a hole chewed about the size of a quarter in the side . . . THERE WAS A HOLE IN MY CLOTHES BAG! From one crisis to another.

I sprang out of bed, grabbed the bag and zipped it open. There beneath shaving kit and Levi's and a packet of bamboo pens were my emergency rations: a box of bittersweet chocolate and several packs of cheese and crackers. One square of chocolate had been half eaten and one cheese section of a cheese-and-crackers box had been consumed. The crackers were untouched.

The mouse. That mouse from last night, under the tool-kit. My little buddy, the one whose life I saved from Hansen's savagery. That mouse had eaten my emergency rations!

"You little devil!" I said fiercely, through gritted teeth.

"What's the matter?" Hansen smoked his cigarette, and didn't turn over.

"Nothing. Mouse ate my cheese."

There was a great burst of smoke from the far couch. "THE MOUSE? That mouse from last night that I said we'd better throw outside? And you felt sorry for him? That mouse ate your food?"

"Some cheese, and a little chocolate, yeah."

"How'd he get at it?"

"He ate a hole through my clothes bag."

Hansen didn't stop laughing until quite a while later.

I drew on heavy wool socks and my boots with the survival knife sewn to the side. "Next time I see that mouse around my clothes bag," I said, "he gets six inches of cold steel, I guarantee ya, no questions asked. Last time I stick up for any mouse. You think at least he'd eat your crazy hat, Hansen, or Stu's toothpaste or somethin', but *my cheese!* Man! Next time, baby, cold steel!"

At breakfast, we dined on Mary Lou's French toahst for the last time.

"We're on our way today, Mary Lou," Paul said, "and you didn't come out and fly with us. You sure missed a good chance. It's pretty up there, and now you'll never know what the sky is like, first hand."

She smiled a dazzling smile. "It's pretty up there," she said, "but it's a silly bunch that lives in it." So that is what our enchantress thought of us. I was, in a way, hurt.

We paid our bill and said goodbye to Mary Lou and rode out to the airport in Al's pickup.

"Think you guys could get back around this way July sixteen-seventeen?" he asked. "Firemen's Picnic, then. Be lots of people here love to have an airplane ride. Sure like to have you back up here."

We began packing our mountain of gear back into the airplanes. The wings of the Luscombe rocked as Paul tied his camera boxes firmly to the framework of the cabin.

"Never can tell, Al. We got no idea where we're gonna be, then. If we're anywhere around here, though, we'll sure be back."

"Glad to have you, anytime."

It was Wednesday morning, then, when we lifted off, circling one last time over Al's place and the Café. Al waved and we rocked our wings farewell, but Mary Lou was busy, or had no time for the silly bunch that lived in the sky. I was still sad about that.

And Rio was gone.

And spring changed to summer.

⚑ CHAPTER SIX ⚑

IT CAME TO US as all Midwest towns did, a clump of green trees way out in the middle of the countryside. At first it seemed trees only, and then the church steeples came in sight, and then the fringe-houses and then at last it was clear that under those trees were solid houses and potential airplane passengers.

The town lapped around two lakes and a huge grass runway. I was tempted to fly right on over it, because there were at least fifteen small hangars down there, and lights along the sides of the strip. This was getting pretty far away from the traditional hayfield of the true barnstormer.

But The Great American Flying Circus was low on funds, the strip was less than a block from town, and the cool lakes lay there and sparkled clear in the sun, inviting us. So we dropped down in, touching one-two on the grass.

The place was deserted. We taxied to the gas pit, which was a set of steel trapdoors in the grass, and shut the engines down into silence.

"What do you think?" I called to Paul as he slid out of his airplane.

"Looks good."

"Think it's a bit too big to work?"

"Looks fine."

There was a small square office near the gas pit, but it was locked. "This is not my idea of a barnstormer's hayfield."

"Might as well be, for all the people around here."

"They'll be comin' out about suppertime, like always."

An old Buick sedan rolled out toward us from town, lurching heavily over the grass driveway to the office. It stopped, and a spare, lined man eased out, smiling.

"You want some gas, I guess."

"Could use some, yeah."

He stepped up on the wooden porch and unlocked the office.

"Nice field, you got here," I said.

"Not bad, for bein' sod."

Bad news, I thought. When the owner doesn't like sod, he's looking for a concrete runway, and when he's looking for a concrete runway, he's looking to make money on business planes, not barnstormers.

"What were you boys doin', tryin' to see how close you could come without hitting?" He touched a switch that set the gas pump to humming.

I looked at Paul and thought I-told-you-so; we don't want to have anything to do with this place.

"Just a bit of loose formation flying," Paul said. "We do it every day."

"Every day? What are you boys doing? You part of an air show?"

"Sort of. We're just barnstormin' around," I said. "Thought we might stay here a few days, hop a few passengers, get people out to look at the airport."

He thought about this for a while, considering implications.

"This is not my field, of course," he said while we gassed

the airplanes and added some quarts of oil to the engines. "Owned by the city and run by the club. I couldn't make the decision by myself. I'd have to call a meeting of the directors. Could do that tonight and maybe you could come on down and talk to them."

I couldn't remember anything about barnstormers meeting with directors to decide whether or not to work a town. "It's nothin' that big," I said. "Just us two airplanes. We do formation and a few aerobatics, and then Stu here does a little parachute jumpin'. That's about it, and carrying passengers."

"Still have to have the meeting, I'd think. How much do you charge?"

"Charge nothin'. It's all free," I said, reeling the gas hose into the pit. "All we're tryin' to do is make gas and oil and hamburgers on the passenger rides, three dollars a throw."

Somehow I got the idea that the town had been hurt in the past by a troupe of roving sky gypsies. It was a completely different meeting than the normal cheer we had come to expect at smaller towns.

"Joe Wright's the name."

We introduced ourselves around, and Joe got on the phone and called a few of the directors of the Palmyra Flying Club. When he was done, he said, "We'll be getting together tonight; like to have you come on down and talk. Meanwhile, I guess you'd like to get something to eat. Place is just down the way. Give you a ride, if you want, or there's a courtesy car."

I would rather have walked, but Joe insisted and we piled into his Buick and drove. He knew the town well, and gave us a pretty little tour of it on the way to the café. Palmyra was blessed with beautiful grass places; a millpond that was still as a lily-pad and green-reflecting quiet like millponds should be; dirt roads through the country, arched overhead by tall curving trees, and quiet back streets with timeless lapstrake and stained glass and oval strawberry-glass front doors.

Every day's barnstorming made the fact a little clearer . . . the only place where time moves is in the cities.

By the time we arrived at the D&M Truck Stop Café, we were well appraised of the town, whose primary industry was a foundry sheltered back in the trees; and of Joe Wright, who was a kind-thinking volunteer airport-operator. He dropped us at the door and left to do some more calling and meeting-arranging.

"I don't like it, Paul," I said when we had ordered. "Why should we bother with a place if it's gonna be no fun? We're free agents, remember . . . go anywhere we want to. There's eight thousand other places than here."

"Don't be so quick to judge," he said. "What's the matter with going to their little meeting? We just go there and act nice and they'll say fine. Then we don't have any problems and everybody knows we're good guys."

"But if we go to the meeting we hurt ourselves, don't you see? We came out here to get away from committees and meetings, and to see if we could find real people, you know, in the little towns. Just being greasy old barnstormers, free in the air, goin' where we please and when we please."

"Now look," Paul said. "This is a good place, right?"

"Wrong. Too many airplanes here."

"It's close in to town, it has lakes, it has people, OK?"

"Well . . ."

We left it at that, though I still wanted to leave and Paul still wanted to stay. Stu didn't want to take sides, but I thought he leaned to the staying side.

When we walked back to the airplanes, we found a few cars parked, and a few Palmyrans looking into the cockpits. Stu unrolled the FLY $3 FLY signs and we went to work.

"PALMYRA FROM THE AIR, FOLKS! PRETTIEST LITTLE TOWN IN THE WORLD! WHO'S THE FIRST

TO FLY?" I walked toward the parked cars when the cockpit-watchers said they were just browsing. "Are you ready for an airplane ride, sir?"

"Heh-heh-heh-heh." That was the only answer I got, and it very clearly said you poor con man, do you really think I'm stupid enough to go up in that old crate?

The quality of that laugh stopped me cold, and I turned abruptly away.

What a crushing difference between this place and the other little places where we had been so welcome. If our search is for the real people and the true people of America, then we should get out of here now.

"Can you take me for a ride?" A man walking boldly from another car changed my attitude at once.

"Love to," I said. "*Stu!* Passenger! Let's go!"

Stu trotted over and helped the man into the front cockpit while I strapped into the rear one. I was very much at home in this little office, with the board of familiar dials and levers around me, and I was happy there. Stu began cranking the inertia-starter handcrank, the device recognized time and again by farm folk as a "cream separator." Straining at the handle, turning it slowly at first, throwing heavy effort into the steel mass of the geared flywheel inside the cowl, Stu drained pure energy from his heart into the starter. At last, starter flywheel screaming, Stu fell away and called, "CLEAR!" I pulled the starter-engage handle and the propeller jerked around. But it turned for only ten seconds. The propeller slowed, and stopped. The engine didn't fire one single time.

What's wrong, I thought. This thing starts every time; it has never missed starting! Stu looked at me in a glazed sort of shock, that all his torture on the crank had gone for nothing.

I was just shaking my head, to tell him I couldn't understand why the engine didn't fire, when I found the trouble. I hadn't turned the switch on. I was so familiar with the cockpit that I had expected the switches and levers to work by themselves.

"Stu . . . ah . . . hate to say this . . . but . . . I forgot to turn the switch on sorry that sure was a silly thing to do let's crank her one more time OK?"

He closed his eyes, imploring heaven to destroy me, and when that didn't work, he made to throw the crank at my head. But he caught himself in time and with the air of a church martyr, inserted the handcrank once again and began to wind it.

"Gee, I'm sorry, Stu," I said, sitting back in my comfortable cockpit. "I owe you fifty cents for forgetting."

He didn't answer, as he had not the strength to talk. The second time I pulled the engage handle the engine roared awake at once, and the jumper looked at me as one looks at a poor dumb beast in a cage. I taxied quickly away and was airborne a moment later with my passenger. The biplane fell into a pattern for Palmyra at once, with a circling detour to look at one of the lakes and to climb a little higher, for there was no emergency landing field anywhere east of town.

The pattern took ten minutes exactly. Touching down, the biplane swerved for a second as I was thinking about what a pretty grass runway this was. Wake up! she was telling me. Every landing, every takeoff is different, every one! And don't you forget it!

I did quick penance by stomping on a rudder pedal to stop the swerve.

As we taxied in, Paul was taxiing out in the Luscombe with a passenger of his own. My spirits brightened a little. Maybe there was hope for Palmyra, after all.

But that was the end of it for the afternoon. We had watchers, but no more passengers.

Stu collected my rider's money, and walked to the cockpit. "I can't do anything with 'em," he said over the engine-roar. "If they stop and get out of their cars, we get passengers. But if they stay in the cars, they're watchers, and they just aren't interested in flying."

It was hard to believe that we could have all those cars and no more riders, but there it was. The watchers all knew each other, and soon a lively conversation was going on. And the Directors arrived to size us up on their own.

Paul landed, taxied in, and lacking more passengers, shut his engine down into silence. A fragment of talk drifted to us. ". . . he was right over my house!"

"He was right over everybody's house. Palmyra isn't that big."

". . . who told you we were having a meeting tonight?"

"M'wife. Somebody called her and got her all shook up . . ."

Joe Wright came over and introduced us to some of the directors, and we told our story again. I was getting tired of this becoming such a big thing. Why couldn't they tell us right out that we were welcome or not? Just a simple thing like a couple of barnstormers.

"You have any schedule for your shows?" one man asked.

"No schedule. We fly when we please."

"Your airplanes are insured, of course; how much would that be?"

"The insurance on these airplanes is what we know about flying," I said, and I wanted to add, *"fella!"* sarcastically. "There is not one cent of any other kind of insurance; no property damage, no liability." Insurance, I wanted to say, is not a signed scrap of paper. Insurance is knowing within us about the sky and the wind, and the touch of the machines that we fly. If we didn't believe in ourselves, or know our airplanes, then there was no signature, no amount of money in the world that could make us secure, or make our passengers safe. But I simply said, again, ". . . not one penny of insurance."

"Well," he paused, startled. "We wouldn't want to say that you're not *welcome* . . . this is a public field . . ."

I smiled, and hoped that Paul had learned his lesson. "Where's the map?" I asked him fiercely.

He had a there-there tone as I stalked to the biplane. "Now look. It's dark almost, and they're going to have their meeting, and we can't go anywhere now so we might as well stay the night and move on tomorrow morning."

"We no more belong here than we belong barnstorming at Kennedy International, man. We . . ."

"No, just listen," he said. "They have a flight breakfast coming up here Sunday. They promised to have a Cessna 180 in here, carrying passengers. Little while ago I heard somebody say that the 180 cancelled out, so they have no one to carry passengers. And here we come. I think after this meeting they're having now, they're going to want us to stay. They're in a bind, and we can help them."

"Shame *on* ya, Paul. By Sunday we'll be in Indiana. Sunday is four days away! And the last thing I want to do is help them out at their flight breakfast. I tell you, we don't belong here! All they want around here is the little tricycle-gear modern airplanes that you drive like a car. Man, I want to be an *airplane* pilot! What the heck's the matter with you, anyway?"

I took a grease rag and began wiping down the engine cowl in the dark. If the biplane had lights I would have flown away that minute.

After a while, the meeting in the office broke up and everyone was hearty and kind to us. I was immediately suspicious.

"Think you boys could stay over till Sunday?" a voice said, out of a crowd of directors. "We're having a little flight breakfast then, be hundreds of airplanes here, thousands of people. You stand to make a lot of money."

I had to laugh. So this is what it felt like to be judged by our vagabond appearance. For just a moment, I was sorry for these people.

"Why don't you stay in the office tonight, boys?" another voice said, and then in a lower tone to someone close by, "We'll take inventory of the oil in there."

I didn't catch the implication of the last sotto voce, but Paul did, at once. "Did you hear that?" he said, stunned. "Did you hear that?"

"I think so. What?"

"They're going to count the oil cans before they trust us in the office. They're going to count the oil cans!"

I replied to whoever had offered the office. "No thanks. We'll sleep out."

"Love to have you stay in the office, really," came the voice again.

"No," Paul said. "We wouldn't be safe there with all your oil cans. You wouldn't want to trust us around all that expensive oil."

I laughed again, in the dark. Hansen, our champion of Palmyra and its people, was furious now at their slur to his honesty.

"I leave fifteen hundred dollars' worth of cameras unlocked in my plane while we go and eat, trusting these guys, and they think we're going to steal a can of *oil!*"

Stu stood quietly by, listening, and said not a word. It was full dark over supper at the D&M before Paul was cool again.

"We're trying to find an ideal world," he said to Joe Wright, who was brave enough to join us. "All of us have lived in the other world, the cutthroat, cheap world, where the only thing that matters is the almighty buck. Where people don't even know what money means. And we've had enough of that, so we're out here living in our ideal world, where it's all simple. For three bucks we sell something priceless, and with that we get our food and gas so we can go on." Paul forgot his fried chicken, he was talking so hard to the Palmyran.

Why are we working on Joe, why are we justifying ourselves to him? I thought. Aren't we sure, ourselves? Maybe we're just so sure that we want to turn a few converts our way.

Our missionary effort, however, was wasted on Joe, who gave little sign that there was anything new or meaningful in what we said.

Stu did nothing but eat his supper. I wondered about the person within the boy, what he thought, what he cared about. I would liked to have met him, but for now, he was listening . . . listening . . . not saying a word, not offering a single thought to the roar of ideas going on about him. Well, I thought, he's a good jumper and he's thinking. There's not much more we could ask.

"I'll drive you back out to the office, if you want," Joe said.

"Thanks, Joe," Paul said. "We'll take you up on that, but we're not going to stay in that office. We'll sleep under the wing. If somebody counted the oil wrong, and then counted it right, after we were gone, you see, we'd automatically be thieves. It's better for us to have that place all locked up and us sleeping out under the wing."

In half an hour, the biplane was a huge silent arrangement of black over our sleeping bags and above the black was the bright mist of the Milky Way.

"Center of the galaxy," I said.

"What's that?"

"Milky way. That's the center of the galaxy."

"It makes you feel kind of small, doesn't it," Paul said.

"Used to. Not so much any more. Guess I'm bigger now."

I chewed a grass stem. "What do you think now? We gonna make money here or not?"

"We'll just have to wait it out."

"I think it's going to work all right," I said, an optimist under the stars. "Can't imagine anybody not coming out to see old airplanes, even in this town."

I watched the galaxy, with its northern cross like a big kite in a wind of stars, sparkling on and off. The grass was soft beneath me, my boots made a firm leathery pillow.

"We'll find out tomorrow." It fell silent under the wing, and the cool wind moaned low in the wires above us, between the biplane's wings.

Tomorrow dawned in fog, and I woke to the slow cannon-boom of fog-drops falling from the top wing down onto the drum-fabric of the bottom one. Stu was awake, quietly rolling a new drift-streamer out of twenty yards of crepe paper. Paul was asleep, his hat pulled down over his eyes.

"Hey, Paul. You awake?"

No answer.

"HEY PAUL! YOU STILL ASLEEP?"

"Mmm." He moved an inch.

"I guess you're still asleep."

"Mm."

"Well, you go ahead and sleep, we won't be flyin' for a while."

"What do you mean?" he said.

"Fog."

The hat was raised by a hand snaking out of the green sleeping bag. "Mm. Fog. Up off the lakes."

"Yeah. Burn off by ten o'clock. Betcha nickel." There was no answer. I tried licking fog from some larger grassblades, but it wasn't much of a thirst-quencher. I rearranged my boot-pillows and tried for a bit more sleep.

Paul came suddenly awake. "Ar! My shirt's all wet! It's soaking wet!"

"Man. City pilots. If I wanted to get my shirt just as wet as I could, I'd lay it out on the wing like you did. You're supposed to put your shirt under your sleepin' bag."

I slid out of my bag and into the dry warm shirt that I had slept on and mashed all kinds of wrinkles into. "Nothing like a nice dry shirt, of a mornin'."

"Ha, ha."

I pulled the cover from the cockpits and unloaded the toolkit and oil cans and FLY $3 FLY sign from the front cockpit. I ragged down the windshields, pulled the propeller through a few times, and in general made ready hopefully for a busy day of barnstorming. The fog was lifting already.

As he finished breakfast, Stu sat back in his chair and stretched his legs. "Shall we try a day jump, see what happens?"

"If you want," Paul said. "Better check with the Leader first." He nodded at me.

"What do you mean? I am always winding up Leader! I'm no leader! No leader! I quit! As Leader, I resign!"

We decided together, then, that it would be good to try a midday jump, to see if anyone was about with time to come and fly.

"Let's not waste any time with freefall stuff," Paul said, "nobody will see you. How about a clear-and-pull from three thousand?"

Stu did not buy this idea. "Rather have time to stabilize a bit. Thirty-five hundred's OK."

"Sounds fine," said Paul.

"If you don't pull, Stu, or your chute doesn't open," I said, "we'll just fly right on to the next town."

"I'm sure it won't make any difference to me," he answered, with a rare smile.

By noon we were airborne, climbing in formation toward the top of the sky. Stu sat in the open door on the right side of Paul's airplane, looking downward, his drift streamer in his hand. As we came near the jump altitude, I broke away and flew some loops and rolls and then clawed my way back up to altitude. There wasn't a person moving anywhere in the streets below. The Luscombe was level on course over the airport, and the long crepe streamer plummeted overboard, slowed to the speed of an open parachute and twisted down toward the grass. It landed several hundred yards west of the target, in the wind.

Way up in Paul's airplane, high over my head, Stu was picking his jump point to correct for the wind, to miss the trees and wires. I stopped cavorting and circled beneath the little sportplane, which by now had nearly reached jump altitude. Paul turned his airplane onto the jump run, into the wind, and we all waited. The Luscombe droned along at a walk; only if I watched carefully could I tell that it was moving at all. And then Stu MacPherson jumped.

A tiny black speck, moving instantly at high speed and straight down, his body turned left, stabilized, turned right, tumbled end over end. I blinked again at the speed of it. In seconds he was no longer a black speck, but a man streaking down through the air, a falcon striking.

Time stopped. Our airplanes were frozen in the air, the sound and the wind were still. The only motion was that sizzling speed of the man whom I last saw crushing himself into the tiny right seat of the Luscombe, and he was moving at least 150 miles per hour toward the flat unmoving earth. In the silence, I could hear him fall.

Stu was still above me when he brought both arms in close to his body, flung them out again, and the long bright rocket of a parachute streamed from his back. It didn't slow him a bit. The narrow line of the chute simply stopped in the air as the man went streaking on down. Then it caught him. All in an instant the chute burst wide open, closed again, and opened to a soft thistle-fluff under which the man floated, still above me.

Time fell back into gear at once, and Paul and I were airplanes flashing again through the sky, the earth was round and warm, and the only sound was the roar of wind and engine. The slowest thing in sight was the orange-and-white canopy drifting down.

Paul arrived in the Luscombe, at high speed, and we circled the open chute, one of us on each side of our jumper. He waved, spun his canopy around, slipped heavily into the wind, which was stronger than he had bargained for. He slipped again, pulling down hard on the risers and almost collapsing one side of his canopy.

All to no avail. We held our altitude at 500 feet while Stu went on down to smash into a tall field of rye that bordered the runway. It looked soft until the instant he crashed into the ground, and then it looked very hard indeed.

I circled and dived to make one low pass over his head, then followed Paul in to land. I taxied to the edge of the rye and got out of the cockpit, expecting to see the jumper at any moment. He didn't appear. I got out of the airplane and walked into the shoulder-high grass, the sound of the engine fading away behind me. "STU?"

No answer. I tried to remember if I had seen him standing up and waving OK after he landed. I couldn't remember.

"STU!"

There was no answer.

☙ CHAPTER SEVEN ☙

THE RYE-FIELD WAS SET on rolling ground and the tops of the stalks made a waving unbroken carpet, hiding everything but the trees on the quarter-mile horizon. Darn me. I should have marked the place better where he went down. He could be anywhere in here. "Hey! *STU!*"

"Over here . . ." It was a very weak voice.

I thrashed through the tall grain in the direction the voice had come and suddenly broke through to an unconcerned jumper, field-packing his chute. "Man, I thought we lost you there. You OK?"

"Oh, sure. Hit kind of hard. This stuff is deeper than it looks from the air."

Our words were strange and oddly quiet; the grass was a sponge for sound. I couldn't hear the airplane engine at all, and had it not been for the trail I had left, walking in, I would have had no idea where it was.

I took Stu's reserve chute and his helmet and we beat our way through the Wisconsin Pampas.

"Jumper in the Rye," Stu mused.

At last the engine-sound filtered in to us, and a minute later we broke out into the clear short grass of the strip. I threw his gear into the front cockpit and he stood on the wingwalk while we taxied back.

There were four passengers waiting, and a small crowd of spectators wondering what we were going to do next. I flew the passengers, two couples, and that was the end of the mid-day jump experiment. Not bad, for the middle of a weekday.

We tired of the airstrip after a while and ambled through the silent day to Main Street, three blocks long. We were tourists on the sidewalk, looking in the shop windows. There was a poster in the dime-store:

AMERICAN LEGION & FIREMEN'S PICNIC
SULLIVAN, WISC.
Saturday-Sunday, June 25–26
COLORFUL PARADE
Drum and Bugle Corps   Kiltie Kadets
Home made pies!   Sandwiches at all times!
WRESTLING Both Nights
2 out of 3 falls

THE MASK   JOHNNY GILBERT
from parts unknown   Michigan City, Ind.

The Firemen's Picnic would be an exciting time. The wrestlers were shown, in their fighting togs. The Mask was a great mound of flesh, scowling through a black stocking mask. Gilbert was handsome, rugged. There was no question that the conflict between good and evil would be a colossal one, and I wondered if Sullivan, Wisconsin had a good hayfield, in close to the ring.

The dime-store itself was a long narrow room with board-wood floors, and the smell of popcorn and hot paper hung in the air. There were elements of forever: a glass-front counter with its chutes and trays of candy, a worn sheet-metal candy scoop half-buried in Red-Hots, a square glass machine filled with multicolored jawbreakers, and way down at the end of the room, at the point where the long counters converged in the distance, a tiny voice sifted to us: "Can I help you boys?"

We felt almost apologetic for being there, travelers from another century, not knowing that folks don't walk into dimestores in the middle of the day.

"I need some crepe paper," Stu said. "Do you have any wide crepe paper?"

The little tiny lady way off down the rows walked toward us, and walking, she grew. She was a full-size person by the time she reached the paper goods section, and there, surrounded by marble-paper composition folders and nickel Big Gun notebooks, was the material for Stu's wind-drift indicator. The lady looked at us strangely, but said nothing more until she said thank you and we walked bell-jangling through the doorway and out into the sun again.

I needed heavy oil for the biplane, and Stu and I walked out a side street to the implement dealer's. Paul went exploring down another street.

The implement dealer's place was a rough-floored wooden cave, with stacks of tires, bits of machinery and old advertising scattered about. The place smelled like new rubber, and it was very cool inside.

The dealer was a busy man and it was twenty minutes before I could ask if he had any heavy oil.

"Sixty weight, you say? Might have some fifty, but sixty I don't think. What you usin' it for?"

"Got an old airplane here, takes the heavy stuff. Fifty's OK if you don't have sixty."

"Oh, you're the guys with the airplanes. Saw you flyin' around last night. Don't they have any oil at the airport?"

"Nope. This is an old airplane; they don't carry the oil for it."

He said he'd check, and disappeared down a flight of wooden stairs to the cellar.

I noticed, while we waited, a dusty poster stapled high on the planks of the wall: " 'We Can . . . We Will . . . We Must . . .' *Franklin D. Roosevelt.* Buy US War Savings Bonds & Stamps NOW!" There was a picture in stark colored silhouette of an American flag and an aircraft carrier sailing over some precise scalloped water-ripples. It had been nailed to that wall longer than our parachute jumper had existed on the earth.

We browsed among the pulleys, the grease, the lawnmowers for sale, and at last our man returned with a gallon can of oil.

"This is fifty, best I could do you. That OK?"

"Fine. Sure do thank you."

Then for $1.25 I bought a can of Essentialube, since there was none of the barnstormer's traditional Marvel Mystery Oil available. *"The Modern Motor Conditioner—It Powerizes,"* the label said. I wasn't sure that I wanted the Wright to be powerized, but I had to have something for top-cylinder lubrication, and this promised that, as well.

Our rule said that all gas and oil was paid from Great American money, taken off the top before we split the profits, so I made a note that the Great American owed me $2.25, and I paid it out of pocket.

By the time we got back to the airport, there were two cars of spectators on the field.

Stu laid out his chute for packing, and I wanted to learn something about it, so Paul took the time to fly two young passengers in the Luscombe. It was a good feeling, to see Paul flying and making money for us while we worked with the thin nylon.

For once Stu talked and I listened.

"Pull out the line guide, will you . . . yeah, the thing with the angle-iron on it. Now we take all the lines from these risers . . ."

The packing of a parachute was a mystery to me. Stu took

great care to show how it all was done, the laying of the suspension lines (". . . we don't call them shroud lines anymore. I guess that's too scary . . ."), the flaking of the panels into one long neat skinny pyramid, the sheathing of the pyramid into the sleeve, the folding of corners that somehow is supposed to prevent friction burns during opening, and the smashing of the whole thing down into the pack.

"Then we just slip the ripcord pins in like . . . so. And we're ready to jump." He patted the pack and tucked in some loose flaps of material with the packing paddle. Then he was the laconic Stu once again, asking tersely if we might be running another jump again this afternoon.

"I don't see why not," Paul said, walking into earshot and casting an appraising eye at the finished pack. I wondered if he was tempted to jump again. It had been years since he had quit, a battered sky-diver after some 230 jumps, grounded with injuries that kept him in a hospital for months.

"Might as well go up right now," he said, "if you promise to come a little closer to the target."

"I'll try."

Five minutes later they were off in the Luscombe, and I was watching from the ground, holding Paul's movie camera and charged with the job of getting some good shots of the jump.

In the zoom-lens viewfinder, Stu was a tumbling black dot, stabilizing in a cross, turning a huge diving spiral one way, pausing, turning the other way. He was in complete control of his body in flight; he could go any direction, I thought, but up. He fell for nearly twenty seconds, then his arms jerked in, and out, pulling the ripcord, and the chute snapped open. The sound of the nylon firing open was a single shot from a 50-caliber pistol. As loud and sharp as that.

Like every jumper, Stu lived for the freefall part of the jump, that bare twenty seconds in a twenty-four-hour day.

He was now "under canopy," which term must be spoken in a very bored tone, for the *real* jump is over, although there is 2000 feet yet to fall, and some delicate handling still to do of a cloth flying machine that is 28 feet wide and 40 feet tall.

He was tracking well, coming right down toward me as I stood by the windsock. I filmed the last hundred feet of the jump and his touchdown, moving back to keep his boots out of Paul's expensive lens.

A jumper, I saw in the viewfinder, is moving at a pretty good clip at that moment he crashes into the ground. I felt the world shudder as Stu hit, 20 feet away. The canopy drifted down to catch me, but I dodged north. I was proud of Stu, suddenly. He was part of our little team, he had courage and skill that I didn't have, and he worked like a professional, a seasoned jumper, though there were only twenty-five jumps in his log.

"Pretty nice, kid."

"At least I didn't get off in the rye-patch." He slipped out of the harness and began gathering the suspension lines into a long braided chain. A moment later Paul landed and walked over to us.

"Man, I really burned off the altitude," he said. "What did you think of that slip? I really had her stood up on the wing, didn't I? Coming down like a ROCK! What did you think of that?"

"I didn't see your slip, Paul. I was taking pictures of Stu."

At precisely that moment a girl of six or seven walked into our group, offered a small blank book, and shyly asked Stu for his autograph.

"Me?" Stu said, stunned to be on stage and in the center of the spotlight.

She nodded. He wrote his name boldly on the paper and the girl ran off with her prize.

"The STAR!" Hansen said. "Everybody wants to watch

the STAR! Nobody watches my great slip, because the old glory-hound is ON STAGE!"

"Sorry about that, Paul," said Stu.

I made a note to get a box of gold stars at the dime-store and stick them all over everything Stu owned.

The Star laid out his chute at once, and soon was lost in the task of repacking for tomorrow. I walked toward the biplane, and Paul followed.

"No more passengers, this time," he said.

"Quiet before the storm." I patted the biplane. "Want to fly her?"

It was a loaded question. The old Detroit-Parks biplane, as I had told Paul over and over, was the most difficult airplane I had ever learned to fly.

"There's a bit of a crosswind," he said cautiously, giving me a way to withdraw my invitation.

"No problem, if you stay awake on landing," I said. "She's a pussycat in the air, but you got to stay pretty sharp on the landing. She wants to swerve, once in a while, and you have to be right there with the throttle and the rudder to catch her. You'll do a great job."

He didn't say another word, but climbed quickly into the cockpit and pulled on helmet and goggles. I cranked the inertia starter, called "CLEAR!" and fell back while the engine roared into life. It was a strange light feeling to see my airplane start engine with someone else in the cockpit.

I walked around and leaned on the fuselage, by his shoulder. " 'Member to go around and try again if you don't like any landing. You got an hour and a half fuel, so no problem there. If she wants to swerve on you, just give her throttle and rudder."

Paul nodded, and in a burst of power swung the plane about and taxied to the grass strip. I went back and picked up his movie camera, focused down on him with the zoom lens, and watched his takeoff through the viewfinder. I felt as though it was my first solo in the biplane, not Paul's. But there he was, smoothly off the ground and climbing, and I was struck with what a pretty sight the biplane made in the air, and the sweet soft chugging that the Whirlwind made in the distance.

They climbed, turned, swooped gently through the sky as I walked with the camera to the far end of the strip, ready to film the landing. I was still nervous, and felt lonely without my airplane. That was my whole world this summer, circling around up there, and now it was all under the control of someone else. I had just four friends that I would allow to fly that airplane, and Hansen was one of them. So what, I thought. So he breaks the thing up to nothing. His friendship is more important to me than the airplane. The airplane is just a bunch of sticks and wires and cloth, a tool for learning about the sky and about what kind of person I am, when I fly. An airplane stands for freedom, for joy, for the power to understand, and to demonstrate that understanding. Those things aren't destructible.

Paul now had the chance he had been awaiting for two years. He was a good pilot and he was measuring himself against the hardest machine he had ever heard of.

The sound of the biplane went silent, high overhead, and as I watched, she flew through a series of stalls while Paul taught himself how she handled at low speeds. I knew what he would be feeling. The aileron control went to nothing, the elevator was very poor, the control stick was loose and dead now in his hand. The rudder was the best control he had left, but when he would need it most, rolling over the ground after landing, it was useless. It took a good firm rudder pedal and power, rudder and a great blast of wind over it, to make the biplane respond, to keep her from tearing herself to pieces in a twisting smashing groundloop across the grass.

The engine roared back as he tested just how much wind he would need over that rudder. Good boy, I thought, take your time with her.

The last of my nervousness vanished when I realized that what mattered was that my friend met his own special challenge, and found courage and confidence within himself.

He swung around some wide soaring turns and came down low over the grass at high speed. I filmed the pass with his movie camera and wished I could remind him that when he was ready to land, that big huge silver nose would be higher in front of him, so that he wouldn't be able to see ahead. It was like trying to land blindfolded, and he had to do it right, first time out.

How would I feel, in his place? I couldn't tell. Somewhere, a long time ago as I flew airplanes, something clicked in me and I had won a confidence with them. I knew within myself that I could fly any airplane ever built, from glider to jetliner. Whether it was true or not was something that only trying would prove, but the confidence was there, and I wouldn't be afraid to try anything with wings. A good feeling, that confidence, and now Paul was working out there for that same little click within himself.

The biplane swept into the landing pattern, close enough to land on the strip no matter where the engine might fail. It turned toward the grass, slowing, settling gently, evenly, across the trees, across the highway, wires whistling softly with the engine throttled back, across the fence at the end of the strip, eased its glide, settled all smooth, under control. As long as he's under control, he's safe, I thought, and I watched him through the viewfinder, finger down on trigger, driving battery-power to turn the film sprockets.

The touchdown was smooth as summer ice melting, the

wheels slid on the grass before they began to roll. The man made me jealous. He was doing a beautiful job with my airplane, handling it as though it was built of paper-thin eggshells.

They rolled smoothly along, the tail came down into the critical time of landing, when the passengers were wont to wave and turn and smile, and the plane tracked straight through the grass. He had made it. My sigh of satisfaction would no doubt show on the movie screen.

At that moment the bright machine, huge in the zoom lens, began to swerve.

The left wing dipped slightly, the airplane curved to the right. The rudder flashed as Paul slammed the left pedal down. "Power, boy, hit the power!" I said. Nothing. The wing dipped farther down, and in a second it touched the ground in a little shower of flying grass. The biplane was out of control.

I looked away from the viewfinder, knowing that the film would show only a rocking picture of some close blurred grass, but uncaring. Maybe he could still survive, maybe the biplane would come out of the ground-loop in one piece.

There was a very dull *whump*—the left wheel collapsing. The biplane slid sideways for a moment, bending first, then breaking. It pitched forward, and at last it stopped. The propeller swung through one last quick time and buried the tip of one blade in the dirt.

I pointed the camera, still clicking, back onto the scene. Oh, Paul. How long would it be now, to win your confidence? I tried to think of how I would feel, breaking Paul's Luscombe, when he had trusted it to me. It was a horrible feeling, and I stopped imagining at once. I was glad I was me, and not Paul.

I walked slowly over to the airplane. It was worse than the crash at Prairie had been. The long trailing edge of the top wing rippled in wild anguished waves. The fabric of the lower left wing was deeply wrinkled again, the tip down in the dirt. Three struts were torn into angles of agony, screaming that a giant twisting force had grabbed and bent. The left wheel was gone, under the airplane.

Paul hopped out of the cockpit and threw the helmet and goggles down into the seat. I searched for some telling understatement but could come up with nothing that told how sorry for him I was, that he should have to hurt the biplane.

"Win a few, lose a few," was all I could say.

"You don't know," Paul said, "you don't know how sorry . . ."

"Forget it. Not worth worrying about. Airplane's a tool for learning, Paul, and sometimes a tool gets a little bent." I was proud to be able to say that in a calm voice. "All you do is straighten it out again and go back flying."

"Yeah."

"Nothing happens by chance, my friend." I was trying to convince myself more than Paul. "No such thing as luck. A meaning behind every little thing, and a meaning behind this. Part for you, part for me. May not see it all real clear right now, but we will, before long."

"Wish I could say that, Dick. All I can say now is I'm sorry."

The biplane looked like a total wreck.

CHAPTER EIGHT

WE DRAGGED THE AIRPLANE, all limp-winged, into the lee of a corrugated tin hangar, and barnstorming came to a sudden halt. The Great American Flying Circus was out of business again.

Not counting the bent struts and broken landing gear fitting, two other gear fittings had begun to tear away, a brake arm had been ripped off, the top of the cowl was bent, the right shock absorbers were broken, the left aileron fittings were twisted so that the control stick was jammed hard.

But the hangar next to us was owned by one Stan Gerlach, and this was a very special kind of miracle. Stan Gerlach had been owning and flying airplanes since 1932, and he kept spare bits and pieces of every plane he'd owned since then.

"Look, you guys," he said that afternoon, "I got three hangars here, and in this one I think I got some old struts off a Travelair I used to have. You're free to take anything you find in here can get you flying again."

He lifted a wide tin door. "Over here are the struts, and some wheels and junk . . ." He banged and screeched his way into a waist-high stack of metal, pulling out old welded airplane parts. "This might do for something . . . and this . . ."

Struts were our biggest problem, since it would take weeks to send out for streamlined steel tubing and make up new pieces for the biplane. And the blue-painted steel that he piled on the floor looked almost like what we were looking for. On impulse I took one and measured it against the good interplane strut at the right wing of the Parks. It was a sixteenth of an inch longer.

"Stan! This thing's a perfect fit! Perfect! She'll drop right in there!"

"Will it? That's fine. Why don't you just take that, then, and looksee if there's anything else here you can use."

My hope came flooding back. This was beyond any coincidence. The odds against our breaking the biplane in a random little town that just happened to be home to a man with the forty-year-old parts to repair it; the odds that he would be on the scene when the breaking happened; the odds that we'd push the airplane right next to his hangar, within ten feet of the parts we needed—the odds were so high that "coincidence" was a foolish answer. I waited eagerly to see how the rest of the problem would be solved.

"You're gonna need to pick this airplane up, somehow," Stan said, "get the weight off the wheels while you weld those fittings. I got a big A-frame here, we can set up." He clanked around some more in the back of his hangar and came out dragging a 15-foot length of steel pipe. "It's all back in there; might as well bring it out now. It all fits together."

In ten minutes we had assembled the pipe into a high overhead beam, from which we could hang a winch to lift the whole front half of the airplane. All we lacked was the winch.

"Think I got a block and tackle down at the barn . . . sure I do. You want to go down and pick it up?"

I rode along with Stan to his barn, two miles out of Palmyra. "I live for my airplanes," he said as he drove. "I don't know . . . I really get a kick out of airplanes. Don't know what I'll do when I flunk my physical . . . go on flying anyway, I guess."

"Stan, you don't know . . . you don't *know* how much I thank you."

"Heck. Those struts might as well help you as set out in the hangar. I advertise a lot of this stuff, and sell a lot to guys who need it. Any struts there you can have, but they'd be fifty bucks to a jockey that would just turn around and resell 'em. I got some welding tanks, too, and a torch, and a lot of other stuff there in the hangar that you might be able to use."

We turned off the highway and parked by the side of an old flake-painted red barn. From one rafter hung a block and tackle.

"Thought it might be here," he said.

We took it down, put it in the back of the truck and drove back to the airstrip. We stopped at the airplane, and in the last of the day's sunlight fastened the block to the A-frame.

"Hey, you guys," Stan said, "I got to get goin'. There's a trouble light here in the hangar and an extension cord some-where, and a table and whatever else you can use. Just lock the place up when you leave, OK?"

"OK, Stan. Thanks."

"Glad to help."

We went to work removing the bent struts. When they came away, the wings sagged more than ever and we propped the lower wingtips with sawhorses. By dark, we had the aileron fittings straightened again and the cowl hammered smooth.

After a while we knocked off work and went to supper, locking Stan's hangar behind us.

"Well, Paul, I have to say you sure beat Magnaflux. 'If there's a weak place anywhere in your airplane, folks, Han-sen's Testing Service will find it and break it up for you.'"

"No," Paul said. "I just touched down, you know, and I

said, 'Oh, boy, I got it down!' and ka-*pow!* You know the first thing I thought? Your wife. 'What will Bette think?' First thing."

"I'll call her. Tell her you were thinking of her. 'Bette, Paul was thinking about you today while he was tearing the airplane all up.' "

We ate in silence for a while, then Paul brightened. "We made some money today. Hey, treasurer. How much money did we make today?"

Stu put down his fork and pulled out his wallet. "Six dollars."

"But there's some Great American money comes off the top," Paul said. "I paid out the quarter to the boys who found the drift marker."

"And I bought the crepe paper," Stu said. "That was sixty cents."

"And I got the oil," I said. "This is gonna be interesting."

Stu paid us our two dollars each, then I put in a claim for their share of the oil money, seventy-five cents each. But I owed Paul eight and a third cents for my share of the wind-drift recovery fee and I owed Stu twenty cents for the crepe paper. So Stu paid eight cents to Paul, deducted the twenty cents I owed him from his bill to me, and handed me fifty-five cents. Paul took my eight cents off his bill and owed me sixty-seven cents. But he didn't have the change, so he gave me fifty cents and two dimes and I gave him two pennies. Tossed 'em into his coffee saucer, is what I did, clinking.

We sat at the table with our little piles of coins, and I said, "We all square? Speak now or forever hold . . ."

"You owe me fifty cents," Stu said.

"Fifty cents! Where do I owe you fifty cents?" I said. "I owe you nothin'!"

"You forgot to turn on the switch. After I cranked myself

to death on the crank, you forgot to turn on the switch. Fifty cents."

Was that just this morning? It was, and I paid.

Joe Wright had stopped by to insist that we sleep in the office. There would be no oil-can count.

There were two couches, but we piled all our equipment inside the building, and our sleeping place again looked more like an airplane factory than an office bedroom.

"You know what?" Paul said, lying in the dark, smoking a cigarette.

"What?"

"You know, I wasn't ever scared that I was going to get hurt? The only thing I was scared of was that I might hurt the airplane. I sort of knew the airplane wouldn't let me get hurt. Isn't that funny?"

The future of the Great American depended upon a pilot, jumper, mechanic, and friend, all of them named Johnny Colin, who had flown with us at Prairie du Chien and worked the miracle of repairing the biplane after its crash there.

That next afternoon at three, Paul fired up the Luscombe and took off west, toward Apple River, where Johnny had his own airstrip. If everything worked to plan, he would be back before dark.

Stu and I tinkered around the airplane, finishing everything we could before the welding had to be done, and at last there was nothing more to do. Everything turned on whether Paul would return with Johnny in the Luscombe.

Stan came out after a time and wheeled out his Piper Pacer for an afternoon flight. A tricycle-gear Cherokee landed, turned around, took off again. It was a quiet afternoon at a little airport.

A car stopped by the wingtip and some Palmyrans stepped out that we recognized from the day before.

"How's it going?"

"Going OK. A little welding and she'll be all ready to put back together again."

"Looks kind of bent, to me, still." The woman who spoke smiled wryly, to say that she meant no hurtful thing, but her friends didn't notice.

"Don't be so hard on 'em, Duke. They've been working out here all day long on this poor old airplane."

"And they'll be flying it again, too," said Duke.

She was a strange woman, and my first impression was that she was a thousand miles away and that this part of her that was living in Palmyra, Wisconsin, was just about ready to speak some mystic word and disappear.

When Duke talked, everyone listened. There was an aura of faintest sadness about her, as though she was of some lost race, captured as a child and taught in our ways, but always remembering her home on another planet.

"This all you fellows do for a living, fly around and give airplane rides?" she said. She looked at me with a level gaze, wanting to know the truth.

"That's pretty well it."

"What do you think of the towns you see?"

"Every one's different. Towns have personalities, like people."

"What's our personality?" she said.

"You're kind of cautious, steady, sure. Kind of careful with strangers."

"Wrong there. This town's a Peyton Place," she said.

Stan came flying down in a low pass over the field and we all watched him whisk by, engine purring.

By now Paul was an hour overdue and the sun was just a little way above the horizon. If he was going to make it, he'd have to be nearly here.

"Where's your friend?" Duke said.

"He's out getting a guy who's a pretty good welder."

She moved to sit on the front fender of the car, a slim alien woman, not unpretty, looking at the sky. I went back to retouching an old patch on the wingtip.

"Here he comes," someone said, and pointed.

They were wrong. The airplane flew right on over, heading toward Lake Michigan, out to the east.

Another airplane appeared after a while and it was the Luscombe. It glided down, touched its wheels to the grass and rolled swiftly by us. Paul was alone; there was no one else in the Luscombe. I turned around and looked at the welding torch. So much for the barnstorming.

"We have lots of airplanes, today," Duke said.

It was an Aeronca Champion, following Paul, and in the cockpit was Johnny Colin. He had brought his own airplane. Johnny taxied right in close to us and shut his engine down. He stepped out of the airplane, unfolding, dwarfing it in his size. He wore his green beret, and he smiled.

"Johnny! Kinda nice to see you."

He picked a box of tools from the back of the Aeronca. "Hi. Paul says he's been workin' on your airplane, keepin' it all bent up for you." He set the tools down and looked at the struts that waited for the torch. "I got to get out pretty early tomorrow, go down to Muscatine, pick up a new airplane. Hi, Stu."

"Hi, Johnny."

"So what's wrong here? This wheel?" He looked down at a broken heavy-steel fitting, and the other work waiting. "That won't be much."

He slipped on a set of black goggles at once and popped his welding torch into life. The sound of that pop was a sound of sheer confidence, and I relaxed. All day long, till that second, I had been carrying myself tense, and now I relaxed. Praise God for such a thing as a friend.

Johnny finished the brake arm in three minutes, touching it with the long welding rod and the razor flame. Then he kneeled by the heavy wheel fitting and in fifteen minutes it was strong again, ready to hold the weight of the airplane. He set Paul to sawing the strut reinforcing pieces to size, while Stu walked through the dusk for food.

One strut was finished by the time Stu came back with hamburgers, hot chocolate and a half-gallon of milk. We all ate quickly, in the shadows of the trouble-light.

Then the torch popped into life again, hissing, the black goggles went down and the second strut was underway.

"You know what he said when I got to his house?" Paul said quietly. "It was right after work, he had just come in, his wife had dinner on the stove. He grabbed that box of tools and he said, 'I'll be back in the morning, I got a broke airplane to fix.' How's that, huh?"

Glowing white, the strut was laid aside, finished, in the dark. Two more jobs to go, and the most difficult of all. Here the torn metal was within inches of the fabric of the airplane, and the fabric, painted heavily with butyrate dope, would burn like warm dynamite.

"Why don't you get some rags, and a bucket of water," Johnny said. "Build us a dam around here. We're workin' pretty close."

The dam was built of dripping rags, and I held it in place while the torch did its job. Squinting my eyes, I watched the brilliant heat touch the metal, turning it all into a bright molten pool, fusing it back together along what had been the break. The water sputtered on the rag dam, and I was tense again.

After a long time, one hard job had been done, and the last one was the worst. It was a heavy bolt carry-through, surrounded by doped fabric and oily wood. Ten inches above the 6,000 degrees of the welding torch, cradled in old dry wood, was the fuel tank. It held 41 gallons of aviation gasoline, just enough to blow the whole airplane about a thousand feet high.

Johnny put out the torch and looked at the situation for a long time, under the light.

"We better be careful on this one," he said. "We'll need the dam again, lots of water, and if you see a fire starting, yell, and throw some water on it."

Johnny and I settled down underneath the airplane, between the big wheels. All the work and fire would be overhead, as we crouched on the grass.

"Stu," I said, "Why don't you get up in the front cockpit there, and watch for anything like a fire, under the gas tank. Take Stan's fire bottle. If you see something, don't be afraid to sing out, and shoot it with the bottle. If it looks like the whole thing is gonna go up, just yell and get the heck out of there. We can lose the airplane, but let's not us get hurt."

It was nearly midnight when Johnny popped the torch on again and brought it overhead, near my dripping dam. The steel was thick, and the work was slow. I worried about the heat going through the metal and firing the fabric beyond the dam.

"Paul, kind of watch over it all, will you, for any smoke or fires?"

The torch, close up, had a tremendous roar, and it sprayed flame like a rocket at launch. Looking straight up, I could see through a narrow slit into the little place beneath the fuel tank. If there was a fire there, we'd be in trouble. And it was hard to see, in the glare and the sound of the torch.

Every once in a while the flame popped back, a rifle-shot, spraying white sparks over us all. The torchfire was buried in smoke where it touched the airplane. It was our own private hell, there under the belly of the biplane.

There was a sudden crackling over my head and I heard Stu say something, faintly.

"PAUL!" I shouted. "WHAT'S STU SAYING? GET WHAT HE'S SAYING!"

There was a flicker of fire overhead. "HOLD IT, JOHNNY! FIRE!" I slammed a dripping rag hard up into the narrow crack overhead. It hissed, in a rolling cloud of steam.

"STU! DARN IT! SPEAK UP! YOU GOT A FIRE UP THERE?"

"OK, now," came the faint voice.

The distance, I thought. The roar of the torch. I can't hear him. Don't be hard on him. But I had no patience with that. We'd all be blown to bits if he didn't make us hear him when there was a fire.

"LISTEN TO 'IM, WILL YA, PAUL? I CAN'T HEAR A WORD HE SAYS!"

Johnny came back in with the torch, and the crackling began overhead, and the smoke.

"That's just grease cookin' off there," he said, next to me.

We lived through three fires in our little hell, and stopped every one of them short of the fuel tank. None of us were sorry, at two a.m., when the torch snapped out for the last time and the gear was finished, glowing in the dark.

"That ought to do it," Johnny said. "You want me to stick around and help you put it back together?"

"No. No problem, here on out. You saved us, John. Let's get some sleep, OK? Man, I don't want to live through that again."

Johnny wasn't noticeably tired, but I felt like an empty balloon.

At 5:30, Johnny and I got up and walked out to his dew-covered Aeronca. He fired the engine coldly awake and put his tools in the back seat.

"Johnny, thanks," I said.

"Yeah. Nothin'. Glad I could help. Now take it easy, please, with that airplane?" He rubbed a clear space in the dew-beads on his windshield, then climbed aboard.

I didn't know what else to say. Without him, the dream would have been twice vanished. "Hope we fly together again soon."

"We'll do it, sometime." He pushed the throttle forward and taxied out into the dim morning. A moment later he was a dwindling speck on the horizon west, our problem was solved, and The Great American Flying Circus was alive again.

CHAPTER NINE

BY FIVE O'CLOCK IN THE AFTERNOON, three days after her second crash of the season, the biplane was a flying machine right out of an old barnstormer's scrapbook: silver patches on her fabric, welded plates on her cabane struts, scorched places and painted-over places.

We went around all the attach points, checking that safety wires and cotter keys were in place, doublechecking jam nuts tight, and then I was back again in the familiar cockpit, the engine ticking over, warming from the quick fires in the cylinders. This would be a test flight for the rigging and for the landing gear welds—if the wheels collapsed on the takeoff roll, or if the wings fell off in flight, we had failed.

I pushed the throttle forward, we rolled, we hopped up into the air. The gear was good, the rigging was good. She flew like a beautiful airplane.

"YA-HOO!" I shouted into the high wind, where no one could hear. "GREAT! LOVE YA, YA OL' BEAST!" The beast roared back, happy.

We climbed on up to 2,000 feet over the lake and flew some aerobatics. If the wings wouldn't fall off with the airplane pulling high G and flying upside-down, they never would. That first loop required a bit of courage, and I double-checked my parachute buckles. The wind sang in the wires like always, and up and over we went, as gently as possible the first time, looking up at the ground over our head, and smoothly back. Then a tighter loop, watching for the wires to start beating in the wind, or struts to bend, or fabric to tear away. She was the same old airplane she had always been. The tightest loop I could put on her, the quickest snap roll, she didn't make a single cry.

We dived back down to the ground, and bounced the wheels hard on the grass during a high-speed run. This was not easy to do, but I had to make it harder on the wheels now than it would ever be with passengers aboard.

She passed her tests, and the last thing left was to see if the rewelding of the gear made any difference in her ground-handling. A tiny misalignment of the wheels could mean an airplane harder than ever to control.

We sailed down final approach, crossed the fence, and clunked down on the grass. I waited with glove ready on the throttle, boots ready on the rudder pedals. She made a little swerve, but responded at once to the touch of throttle. She seemed the faintest bit more skittish on the ground than she had been. We taxied back to Stan's hangar, triumphant, and the propeller windmilled down into silence.

"How is she?" Paul said, the second the engine stopped.

"GREAT! Maybe just a shade on the dicey side, landing, but otherwise, just great." I jumped down from the cockpit and said what I knew I had to say, because some things are more important than airplanes. "You ready to give her another try, Paul?"

"Do you mean that?"

"I wouldn't say it if I didn't mean it. If she's bent again, we'll fix her again. You ready to go?"

He thought for a long moment. "I don't think so. We

wouldn't be getting much barnstorming done, if I hurt her again. And we're supposed to be out here to barnstorm, not to fix airplanes."

It was still light, in the afternoon of a Saturday.

"Remember how you said if it was right for us to be here Sunday, nothing could keep us away?" Paul said. "Looks like it was right for us to be here Sunday, unless you want to bug out tonight."

"Nope," I replied. "Sunday here is fine. The only way I could have been forced to be here was just the way it happened. So I figure that something interesting is waiting for us tomorrow."

Sunday morning was the Annual Palmyra Flight Breakfast, and the first airplanes began arriving at seven a.m. By seven-thirty we had carried our first passengers, by nine we had both airplanes flying constantly and a crowd of fifty people waiting to fly. A helicopter was carrying passengers at the other side of the field. Our crowd was twice as large as his, and we were proud.

The air cluttered up with little airplanes of every modern kind, coming for the giant breakfast that was a tradition at the airport. The biplane and the Luscombe surged in and out of the traffic pattern, passing each other, working hard, snarling at the other airplanes, which were in no hurry to get back on the ground again.

We had learned that it is not wise to fly a landing pattern so far from the field that we could not glide to the runway if the engine stopped, but at Palmyra we were alone in our learning. There were long lines of aircraft all over the sky, and if all the engines stopped at once, there would be airplanes down everywhere except on the airport.

We flew constantly, drinking an occasional Pepsi-Cola in the cockpit while Stu strapped in more riders. We were making money by the basket, and we were working hard for it. Around and around and around. Palmyrans were out in force; most of our passengers were women and most of them were flying for the first time.

I watched the high wind of flight buffet and blow forward over graceful sculptured faces and was astonished again that there could be so many attractive women in one small town.

The flights fell into a solid pattern, not only in the air, but in our thought.

Buckle the belt down tight on them, Stu, and don't forget to tell them to hold their sunglasses when they look over the side. Taxi out here, careful of other airplanes, recheck the final-approach path for anyone else coming in. Swing onto the grass runway, stay sharp on the rudder here and see if you can lift off right in front of our crowd, so they can see the bright crosses on the wheels spin around, after the biplane is in the air. If we lose the engine now, we can still land on the runway. Now, and we shoot for the meadow beyond. Up over the farm, a little turn so they can look down on the cows and the tractor, if we lose the engine now there's a fine little field across the road. Level at 800 feet, swing out to circle Blue Spring Lake. We sure are making a lot of money today. I have lost track of the passengers . . . at least two hundred dollars today, for sure. But you really work for it. Watch for other airplanes, keep looking around, lose the engine now and we land right across from the lake; nice flat place there to come down. Turn now so the folks can see the sailboats out in the breeze, and motorboats and skiers pulling white trails across the lake. A place to land over there on the left, one more circle here, throw that in for free to give them one last long look at the blueness of that lake, then down across the green meadow into the landing pattern and over town look out now there are all kinds of airplanes around. Fall into place behind the Cessna . . . poor guy doesn't know what he's missing not having an open-cockpit airplane to fly; has to drive around in that milk-stool. Of course he can get places twice as fast as we can and that's what he wants, so fine, I guess. Wish he would keep his pattern closer, though, someday his engine will stop in the pattern and he's gonna feel pretty dumb, not able to glide to the runway. There he's in, turn here, slip off some altitude, look at the wind again, crosswind, but no problem. Aim for the right side of the runway and plan to cut in toward the center so we'll be slow enough by our crowd and ready to pick up more passengers boy the old barnstormers worked for their keep, forget it, it's time to land now and every landing's different remember stay sharp and awake you sure would look dumb groundlooping in front of a crowd like this, even if you didn't hurt the airplane. Wheels are stronger than ever, good ol' Johnny can really weld, that guy, and a better friend you aren't gonna find anywhere. Ease her down, now, across the fence, those cars better look out for airplanes, driving by there, and we're down and this is the hardest part of the whole thing keep her straight, straight, wait on the throttle, on the rudder they're glad they're down but they liked the ride, too. Slow and swing around in toward Stu let 'em out careful boy and keep them from stepping on the fabric and two more ready to fly, the brave people overcoming their fears and trusting me just because they want to see what it looks like from the air. A mother and her daughter this time, they don't know it yet, but they're going to like flying, too. Buckle the belt down tight on them, Stu, and don't forget to tell them to hold their sunglasses when they look over the side . . .

Over and over and over again.

But once, the pattern changed, and while Stu was loading passengers, an angry man came to stand beside my cockpit. "I know you're a hot pilot and all that," he said venomously, "but you might be careful in the landing pattern for a change.

I was coming down final in the twin there, the Apache, and you cut me right out, you turned right in front of me!"

My first thought was to say how sorry I was to do such a thing, but then his attitude struck me. Would I act like that to a fellow pilot on a crowded day? For some distant reason I remembered a pilot named Ed Fitzgerald, back with the 141st Tactical Fighter Squadron, USAF. Fitz was one of the finest pilots I knew, and a staunch friend, but he was the fiercest man in the Air Force. He always frowned, and we said that he was spring-loaded to the *explode* position. If a man made the mistake of crossing Fitz in any tiny way, he had to be ready for hand-to-hand combat with a wild leopard. Even if he was wrong, Ed Fitzgerald wouldn't wait a second to slap down a stranger that dared antagonize him.

So I thought of Fitz then, and smiled within myself. I stood up in the cockpit, which made me a yard taller than this Apache pilot, and frowned down at him, furiously, as Fitz would have done.

"Look here, buddy," I said. "I don't know who you are, but you're flying the pattern in a way's gonna kill somebody. You drag all over the country and then turn toward the airport and expect everybody to get out of your way 'cause you got two engines on your crummy airplane. Look, buddy, you fly like that and I'll cut you out of the pattern every time; you go up there now and I'll cut you out again, you hear me? When you learn to fly an airplane and fly the pattern, then you come back and talk to me, huh?"

Stu had finished strapping the passengers in and I pushed the throttle forward, to press the man off balance with the propeller-blast. He stood back, mad, and I pulled my goggles down and taxied off in a windstorm impossible to answer. I laughed all the way out to takeoff. Good ol' Fitz, come back to help me.

By three o'clock the field was just as empty and quiet as it

had been all the rest of the year. There was not another airplane in sight, save the Luscombe and the biplane. We walked
across the cornfield to lunch, and collapsed at our table.

"Three hamburgers and three Barnstormer Specials, Millie." Another aspect of security. You not only know the waitress, you have your own table and add things to the menu.
Our table was for three, against the side wall, and the
Barnstormer Special was strawberry sherbet with Seven-Up,
whipped on the malt machine. Stu had even written it down,
and it might still be there on a menu in Palmyra.

After a long time, Paul spoke, rubbing his eyes. "What a
day."

"Mm," I agreed, unwilling to make the effort to open my
mouth.

"What's with Duke?" Stu said, after a moment, and when
it was clear that nobody was going to do much talking, he
went on. "She was out there all day watching you guys fly,
but she never bought a ticket. Says she's scared."

"That's her problem," I said.

"Anyway, we are invited over with her and some of her
friends for dinner tonight. Right across from the lake. Do
we want to go?"

"Sure we want to go," Paul said.

"Said they'd be back at five, pick us up."

A silence again, which I finally broke. "Does it work? Can
a barnstormer survive?"

"If your bird could survive that groundloop and get flying
again two days later," Paul said, "disaster has been ruled out.
And I don't know how much money we made, but we made a
pile of money. If a guy sat down and scheduled himself so he
could make all the fly-in breakfasts, and all the county fairs
and all the homecomings at little towns, he could buy out
Rockefeller in about a week and a half."

"Long as you keep the airplanes flying, carrying passengers, you're in business," Stu said. He paused a moment. "Duke said today when I was selling tickets that they had a pool going in town, said the biplane would never fly again, after the crash."

"She was serious?" I asked.

"Seemed to be."

"Shows to go ya. You see how the helicopter finally gave up. The old Great American was really rackin' 'em up, and I guess he finally just couldn't stand the competition."

It was silent for a while, then Paul spoke again. "You know, that girl flew with me three times."

"What girl was that?"

"I don't know. She never said a word, she never smiled, even. But she rode three times. Nine bucks. Where does a girl get nine bucks to throw away on airplane rides?"

"Throw away?" I said. "Throw away? Man, the girl's *flyin'!* Nine bucks is *nothin'!*"

"Yeah. But you don't find too many like that, who think that way. And hey, you know what? Two autographs today. I signed two autographs!"

"Nice," I said. "Knocked me over, too. I had one little fella came up and wanted me to sign his book. How about that, Stu? You are no longer the Star."

"Poor Stu," Paul said loftily. "Did you sign any autographs today . . . Star?"

Stu answered softly. "Twelve," he said, and looked away.

By five o'clock we had the airplanes covered for the evening. We could have carried more passengers, but we were not in the mood for it, and closed our airplane-ride stand.

Duke and her friends arrived and drove us out to a house just across from Palmyra's other lake. There was time for a swim, but Paul chose to stay on shore; the water was looking cold.

"Borrow your comb, Stu?" I said after an hour in the lake, when we were back at the house.

"Sure." He handed me a fractured stick of plastic that had five teeth on one end, a long space, a brief forest of 18 teeth, and all the rest empty.

"Jumper's comb, I guess," Stu apologized. "A few hard landings kinda wiped it out."

The comb was not too effective.

We returned to the gathering, a crowd of people in the living room, and munched on sandwiches and potato chips. They were quizzing Paul on what we were up to, barnstorming.

There was a certain wistfulness in the room, as though we had something that these people wanted, that they might have had a distant wish to say goodbye to everything in Palmyra and fly away into the sunset with The Great American Flying Circus. I saw it most of all in the girl Duke. And I thought: if they want to do something like this, why do they wait? Why don't they just do it, and be happy?

Paul, talking with hard logic, had brought Duke around to the idea of a flight in the Luscombe.

"But it's got to be at night," she said.

"Why at night? You can't see nearly so . . ."

"That's just it. I don't want to see. I get this urge to jump. Maybe I won't get it at night."

Paul stood up. "Let's go."

They went. It was solid black outside; an engine failure on takeoff would give him a busy few moments. We listened, and some time later we heard the Luscombe taking off, and then saw its navigation lights moving among the stars. They stayed over town and circled higher. Good for Paul. He wouldn't be caught out of gliding distance to the field.

We talked for a while longer, back in the house, about what a strange girl Duke was; how long she had been afraid to go up in an airplane, and how there she was up there in the middle of the night where no one else would think of flying, first time.

Stu took his licks for not being very talkative, and I found an old ornamental guitar and began tuning it. The E string broke at once, and I was sorry I ever saw the thing. A piece of fishline as an emergency string tuned way too high.

After a while the flyers came back.

"It's beautiful," Duke told us all. "The lights and the stars. But after five minutes I said, 'Take me down, take me down!' I could feel myself wanting to jump."

"She couldn't have jumped out of that airplane if she tried," Paul said. "She couldn't even open the door."

Duke talked for a bit about what it felt like, but in cautious, withdrawn words. I wondered what she really thought.

In an hour we thanked our hosts, bid them goodbye, and walked through the night back to the airstrip.

"I would have been in trouble if the engine quit on take-off." Paul said. "I knew the meadow was out there, but I sure couldn't see it. Man, I was on instruments as soon as we broke ground . . . it was BLACK! I couldn't even tell where the horizon was. That spooky feeling, you know, whether the stars are the town or the town is stars."

" 'Least you stayed in gliding distance, once you got up," I said.

"Oh, once we were up it was no problem at all. Just that one little time right at liftoff."

We tramped into the office, and snapped on the light.

"What a day."

"Hey, treasurer, how much money did we make today?"

"I don't know," said Stu, and he smiled. "We'll count it up tomorrow, boys." Stu was older now than when he joined the circus. He knew us, was the difference, I thought, and I wished we could say the same of him.

"The devil we count it up tomorrow," I said. "Tomorrow we wake up and find our treasurer is on his way to Acapulco."

"Count 'er out, Stu," Paul said.

Stu began emptying his pockets onto the couch from the biggest day's work we'd had all summer. There were great crushed wads of money in all pockets, and his wallet was stuffed with bills. The final pile on the couch was wrinkled and impressive.

Stu counted it into fifty-dollar piles, while we watched. There were seven piles and some bills left over; three hundred and seventy-three dollars. "Not bad, for a day's flyin'," I said.

"Just a minute." Paul said, calculating. "That can't be right. It is three dollars a ride, so how can we come out with a number like 373?"

Stu patted his pockets. "Ah, here's a whole wad I missed," he said, and to a chorus of suspicious mutterings, he counted another seventeen dollars onto the last pile. "Don't know how that could have happened."

"There's our warning, Paul," I said. "We gots to be careful of the treasurer."

There was $390 laid out now, a mirror of 130 passengers, most of whom had never flown before in their lives. You can destroy that pile of bills, I thought, or spend it right up, but you can never destroy the flights that those 130 people had today. The money is just a symbol of their wish to fly, to see far out over the land. And for a moment I, oily barnstormer, felt as if I might have done something worthwhile in the world.

"What about gas and oil? What do we owe on that?"

I checked the tally sheet on the desk and added the figures.

"Comes out to $42.78. We used 129.4 gallons of gas and 12 quarts of oil. We should pay Stan for the stuff of his, too, that we used. Acetylene and oxygen and welding rod and stuff. What do you think? Twenty bucks sound right?" They agreed it did.

Stu was figuring how to split the money four ways, keeping one pile for Johnny Colin. "OK. That makes $81.80 apiece with two cents left over. Anybody want to check my figures?" We all did, and he was right. We put the odd two cents on Johnny's pile, for mailing the next day.

"You know," I said, when we were all rolled up for the night, "maybe it's a good thing we didn't wind up with ten airplanes, or whatever, on this show. The only time we could keep ten airplanes busy flying passengers is a day like this. We'd have starved, ten of us; we couldn't even pay our gas."

"You're right," Paul said. "Two airplanes be about it, maybe three, unless you want to get all organized and follow the county fairs and fly-in breakfasts."

"Can you imagine us organized?" I said. " '*Today, men, we will all fly one eight zero degrees for eighty-eight miles to Richland, where we will all carry passengers from noon to two-thirty. Then we will proceed west for forty-two miles, where we will fly passengers from four o'clock to six-fifteen . . .*' Bad news. Glad it's just us."

"You probably say we're being 'guided,' that the other airplanes just couldn't make it?" Paul said. "And that all these crashes don't stop us?"

"You better believe it, we're being guided," I said. I was growing more confident of this, in the light of our miracles. Yet while Midwest America appeared both beautiful and kind, I still wondered what sudden adventures might next be guided across the path of The Great American Flying Circus. I wasn't quite so eager for adventure, and hoped for a time of calm.

I forgot that calm, for a gypsy pilot, is disaster.

♚ CHAPTER TEN ♚

WE SENT JOHNNY'S MONEY OFF to him the next morning, all cash in a bulky envelope, and a note saying thanks.

Over a late breakfast at the D&M, Paul looked at the list of clients he had promised to photograph.

"I have a company down in Chicago, on the outskirts there. I really should go down and shoot that. Then there's one in Ohio, and Indiana . . . are we going to get to Indiana?"

"You're leader today," I said.

"No, come on. You think we'll ever hit Indiana?"

"Got me. Depends on how the wind is blowing, you know."

"Thanks. I do have to get this Chicago guy, then as long as I'm there I might as well hop over to Indiana. I could join up with you guys again later on, wherever you are."

"OK. I'll leave word with Bette, tell her where we are. You call her, fly in and meet us when you can." I was sorry to have Paul think more of his shooting than of barnstorming, but he was free to do whatever he wanted to do.

We said goodbye to Millie, leaving monster tips on the table, and walked back to the planes. We took off together, stayed in formation up to 800 feet and then Paul waved and banked sharply away toward the distance of Lake Michigan and the 1960's.

We were alone. The Great American Flying Circus was now one biplane and one pilot and one parachute jumper; destination, as always, unknown.

The land below went flat. It began to look like Illinois, and after an hour's flying we saw a river in the distance. There was no other airplane in the sky, and on the ground everyone was working at some kind of reasonable, respectable job. It was a lonely feeling.

We followed the river south and west, the biplane trailing a little stream of roiled air behind it, above the stream of water.

There were few places to land. The fields close to the towns were hemmed in by telephone wires or planted in corn and beans. We flew for several hours in random directions, staying close to the water, and at last, just as I was about to give up in disgust, we found a field at Erie, Illinois. It was short, it had trees across one end, it was half a mile from town. All of these things were bad, but down on the field the hay was being raked and baled and a wide strip had been left clear. We whistled down over a cornfield and landed in the adjoining hay, rolling to a stop not far from where a farmer was working over a huge rotary rake. He was having some trouble with it, and I shut down the engine.

"Hi, there," I said.

"Howdy."

Stu and I walked to the rake. "Can we help you out at all?"

"Maybe. I'm tryin' to get this thing hooked up to the tractor, but it's too heavy."

"Can't be. We can lift that little thing up there." Stu and I lifted the tongue of the rake, which was solid steel, set it in the tractor hitch, and dropped the locking pin down through.

"Thank you kindly, boys," the farmer said. He wore a

denim jacket over his coveralls, a railroad engineer's cap and a manner of unruffled calm at an airplane dropping down into his field.

"You've got a nice hayfield here," I said. "Mind if we fly out of here a bit, carry some passengers?"

"Just one time?"

"Lots of times, we hope."

"Well . . ." He was not sold on the idea, but at last he said it would be all right.

I unloaded the airplane for some trial flights, to see how much clearance we'd have, over the trees. It didn't feel good. We cleared the top branches with much less margin than I had hoped for, and with the weight of passengers aboard, it would not be comfortable. But there was no other field in sight, all the way around town. Everything was corn.

It was no use trying. Our field was just not good enough and we had to move on. By now the sun was low, and so was our fuel. We chose to stay overnight and move out early in the morning. The plan was firmed when the farmer stopped by just at dusk.

"Just as soon you not fly much out of here, boys. Your motor exhaust might hurt m'hay."

"OK. Mind if we stay the night, here?"

"Go right ahead. Just don't want that exhaust to get to the hay, is all."

"Thank y', sir." We began to walk into town for our hamburgers, keeping to the right of the road, scuffing through the weeds.

"What about his tractor?" Stu said. "Doesn't his tractor have an exhaust?"

"Yeah, but it doesn't make any difference. He wants us out of here, we get out. No questions. It's his land."

At sundown we went back to the plane and the sleeping bags. There were ten billion river-mosquitoes waiting for us.

They cruised, humming gently, at low power, and all of them were quite eager to meet us.

Stu, not quite so silent since Paul left, had suggestions. "We could put out a quart of blood for them, on the wing," he said. "Or tether a couple hundred frogs around here. Or we could start the engine and fan them away . . ."

"You're very creative, my lad, but all that's needed is that we come to an understanding with the mosquitoes. They have their place to live in the world, you see, and we have ours . . ."

"We could go back into town and get some repellent stuff . . ."

". . . and as soon as we understand that they don't have to conflict with our peace, why, they'll just . . . go."

At ten o'clock we were walking to town. Every seven minutes, as we walked, a shiny new automobile, without muffler, came blazing out from town at something over 70 miles an hour, stopped, turned around and went blazing back in. "What the devil are these nuts doing?" I said, mystified.

"Dragging Main."

"What?"

"It's called 'Dragging Main,'" Stu explained. "In little towns, the kids have nothing to do, so they just go back and forth, back and forth, in their cars, all night long." He had no comment whether he thought it good or evil. He just told me it was.

"This is entertainment? This is what they do for fun?"

"Yeah."

"Wow."

Another car went shrieking by. No. It was the same car that we had seen seven minutes ago.

Good grief, I thought. Would we have had an Abraham Lincoln, a Thomas Edison, a Walt Disney, if everyone spent their non-school hours Dragging Main? I watched the split-second faces at the wheel, and saw that the young men passing by were not so much driving as being driven, by sheer and desperate boredom.

"I eagerly await the contributions these guys are gonna make to the world."

It was a warm night. Stu knocked on a market door just as it was closing, explained about the mosquitoes, and paid fifty cents for a bottle of promises to keep them away. I bought a pint of orange sherbet, and we walked back to the airplane.

"You want some of this stuff?" Stu asked.

"Nope. All you need is an understanding . . ."

"Darn. I was going to sell you a squirt of it for fifty cents."

Neither one of us reached a peace with the little creatures.

At five-thirty in the morning we were airborne, ghosting southeast over calm rivermist, toward a black mark on a road-map that was supposed to be an airport. We had one hour's fuel on board, and the flight would take 30 minutes.

The air was still as the sun, pushing light up over the cool horizon, and we were the only moving thing in a thousand miles of sky. I could see how an old barnstormer might re-member his days in gladness.

We flew on through a difficult week, surprised at how few were the Illinois towns that could be good homes for gypsy pilots. Our Palmyran profits were gone.

We landed in desperation once, at a grass airport near Sandwich. It was a soft green runway, many thousand feet long, and fairly close to town. We were tired from so much non-profit flying, and even though it wasn't a hayfield, we thought this would be a good place to spend the evening.

The airport office had just been remodeled, was panelled in deep-stained satin wood, and I began to wonder if we be-longed here from the first moment that I saw the owner, by the window. He had watched this grease-spattered biplane land, he had worried about its oil dripping on his grass, and now its filthy occupants were going to *step inside his new office!*

He tried to be polite, that much can be set down for him. But he welcomed The Great American Flying Circus about as warmly as he would have welcomed the Loch Ness Monster to his doorstep.

I told him brightly what we were doing, how we had never carried a dissatisfied passenger, how we could bring many new customers to his field and increase his own passenger-flying business.

"I'm a little on the conservative side," he said when I was through. And then, cagily, "You do your own maintenance?"

To do one's maintenance, without a license, is illegal, and he waited like a vulture for our answer, thinking of the price on our heads. He was disappointed, almost, to hear that the biplane was properly signed and provided for. Then he brightened. "I'm having the opening of the new building next month. I could use you then . . ."

Being used did not sound like much fun. Stu and I looked at each other and moved to leave. At that instant, as in a motion-picture script, a customer walked in the door.

"I want to have an airplane ride," he said.

The owner began a long apologetic explanation about how his flying license was not up to date and it wouldn't be worth it to call out a pilot from town to give just one ride and his airplanes were all down for maintenance anyway. We didn't say a word. We just stood there, and so did the customer. He wanted a ride.

"Of course these fellows could ride you. But I don't know anything about them . . ."

Ah, I thought, the fraternity of the air.

The customer was almost as frightened of the biplane as the airport manager had been, although in a more straightforward way. "I don't want any dadoes, now, no flip-flops. Just take it kind of easy, around town and back down again."

"Gentle as a cloud, sir," I said, with a flourish. "STU, LET'S GET THIS THING FIRED UP!"

The flight was gentle as a cloud, and the man even said that he liked it. A few seconds after we landed, he was gone, leaving me puzzled over why he wanted to go up in the first place.

We were airborne again in fifteen minutes, glad to leave Sandwich and its gleaming new office behind. Droning on north again, aimless, looking down, some of the old doubts about surviving came back to mind.

We landed at last at Antioch, a resort town a few miles south of the Wisconsin border. The grass field lay on the edge of a lake and we found that the owner sold rides on weekends in his Waco biplane. He charged five dollars the ride, and he was not interested in any competition, any time, and he would be happiest if we would leave. But before we could go, a modern Piper Cherokee landed and taxied to our side. A businesslike fellow in white shirt and tie walked purposefully toward us and smiled in the way of a man whose job forces him to meet many people.

"I'm Dan Smith," he said over the engine noise, "Illinois Aeronautics Commission."

I nodded, and wondered why he had made such a big thing of his title. Then I saw that he was looking for an Illinois State Registration tag on the biplane. He hadn't found one. The tag is a mandatory thing in that state. It costs a dollar or so, which apparently pays the field worker's salary.

"Where are you from?" he asked.

From anyone else, a normal, harmless question. From this man, it was sinister. If I'm from Illinois, I'm fined on the spot.

"Iowa," I said.

"Oh."

Without another word, he walked to the hangar across the way and disappeared within it, checking for hidden airplanes, without registration tags.

What a way to make a living, I thought.

Airborne again, we were getting desperate. In all this lake country, we could find no place to land near a lake. Simple criteria, we had: near town, near lake. But there was no such thing. We circled for more than an hour over a score of lakes, and found nothing. Thirst had a sharp edge, there in the high hot cockpits, and we flew north again, looking for any place to land.

We crossed Lake Geneva and looked down thirstily at all that water. Water skiers, sailboats, swimmers . . . drinking as much of the lake as they wanted.

The first airstrip we saw, we landed. It was the wrong place. *Lake Lawn,* a bright sign said. The grass was immaculately trimmed, and we discovered that this was the private airstrip of the Lake Lawn Country Club.

Parking the greasy biplane out of sight, we snuck out of the cockpits and walked down the road toward the Club after the manner of working gardeners. The guards at the gate caught us, but had compassion and showed us the way to water.

"I'm beginning to doubt your method of finding fields," Stu said.

Then we were up again, grimly heading south in the third giant circle of the week. There is no such thing as chance, I thought, gritting my teeth, there is no such thing as luck. We were being led where it is best for us to go. There is a good place waiting, this minute. Just ahead.

A long open summer field slanted beneath us, far from any town, but a fine place for airplanes to land.

I thought about landing there and giving rides to the cows

grazing about. For a half-second I was serious, wondering if it could work. It always came back to this. We had to prove it all over again, every day . . . we had to find human, paying passengers.

❧ CHAPTER ELEVEN ❧

THE TOWN OF WALWORTH, Wisconsin, is a fine and friendly place. It showed that friendliness by spreading before us a smooth soft hayfield, all mowed and raked. The field was three blocks from the center of town, it was long and wide, and the approaches were good save for one set of low telephone wires. We landed, on our last reserves of money and morale.

The owner of the field was kind, mildly amused at the old airplane and the strange people who came down from it. "Sure you can fly out of the field, and thanks for the offer of a ride. Take you up on it." Hope stirred. Somebody had said we were welcome!

The signs were out in a flash, and we flew two free rides for the owner and his family. By sundown, we had flown three paying rides, as well. That evening, the treasurer informed me that on this day we had paid $30 for gasoline, but that we had taken in $12 from passengers. Clearly, our fortunes were changing.

Gazing back at me in the morning from the gas station mirror was a horrible image, a scraggly rough-bearded Mr.

Hyde so terrible that I drew back in alarm. Was that me? Was that what the farmers had seen whenever we landed? I would have run this monster off with a pitchfork! But the bearded image disappeared at last to my electric shaver, and I felt almost human when I walked again into the sunshine.

We had to make money at Walworth, or quit. We reviewed the ways we had to bring customers; Method A, flying aerobatics at the edge of town. Method B, the parachute jump. Then we began experimenting with Method C. There is a principle that says if you lay out a lonely solitaire game in the center of the wilderness, someone will soon come along to look over your shoulder and tell you how to play your cards. This was the principle of Method C. We unrolled our sleeping bags and stretched out under the wing, completely uncaring.

It worked at once.

"Hi, there."

I lifted my head at the voice and looked out from beneath the wing. "Hi."

"You fly this airplane?"

"Sure do." I got to my feet. "You lookin' to fly?" For a fleeting moment, the man looked familiar, and he looked at me with the air of one who was trying to remember. "It's a nice flight," I said. "Walworth's a pretty little town, from the air. Three dollars American, is all."

The man read my name from the cockpit rim. "Hey! You're not . . . Dick! Remember me?"

I looked at him again, carefully. I had seen him before, I knew him from . . . "Your name is . . ." I said. What was his name? He rebuilt an airplane. He and . . . Carl Lind rebuilt an airplane a couple of years ago . . . "Your name is . . . Everett . . . Feltham. The Bird biplane! You and Carl Lind!"

"Yessir! Dick! How the heck you been?"

Everett Feltham was a flight engineer for some giant airline. He had been brought up on Piper Cubs and Aeronca Champs, was an airplane mechanic, pilot, restorer. If it flew through the air, Everett Feltham knew about it; how to fly it and how to keep it flying.

"Ev! What are you doin' here?"

"I live here! This is my home town! Man, you never can tell what kind of riff-raff gonna fall down on you from the sky! How's Bette? The children?"

It was a good reunion. Ev lived only two miles north of the field we had landed in, and our friend Carl Lind kept a country house on Lake Geneva, ten miles east. Carl had flown airplanes in the late twenties, barnstorming around this very countryside. He quit flying when he married and raised his family, and he was now the president of Lind Plastic Products.

"A gypsy pilot," Ev said. "Might have known it was you, doing a crazy thing like this, landing in a hayfield. You know there's an airport just down the road."

"Is there? Well, it's too far out. You got to be close to town. We're a bit in the hole after flyin' around all week for nothin'. We got to get some passengers up in the air this afternoon or we'll be starvin' again."

"I'll call Carl. If he's home, he's gonna want to come out and see you, probably want you over to the house. You need anything? Anything I can bring you?"

"No. Rags, maybe—we're runnin' out of rags. If you got some around."

Ev waved and drove away, and I smiled. "Funny thing about flying, Stu. You can never tell when you're gonna run into some old buddy somewhere. Isn't that somethin'? Go land in a hayfield, and there's ol' Ev." Nothing by chance, nothing by luck, the voice, almost forgotten, reminded.

After suppertime, the passengers started coming. One woman said the last time she had flown was when she was six

The Luscombe and the biplane in earlier days, as we were practicing landings in fields, wondering if it just might be possible to survive as modern-day barnstormers.

Sometimes it is devilish hard to pick up a handkerchief.

And sometimes it's easy.

How it looks after you hit the thing, and climb away in triumph. That's a smoke flare tied to the horizontal stick, which I could fire by pressing a button in the cockpit.

When you smash a wheel into a dike of earth at 110 miles per hour, you expect some inconvenience.

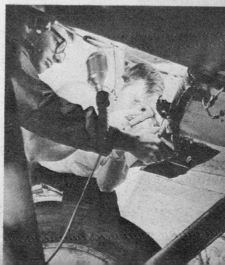

The beauty of friends, Part 1. Stu MacPherson and Johnny Colin, having welded the broken landing gear, begin on the wing. I've gone to Iowa after a spare propeller.

Part 2. Johnny, Dick Willetts, Stu and Paul Hansen worked through the rain to fix the biplane while I was gone. Paul took this picture (and all the others, too).

The last bits of repair, and Johnny is all set, drift streamer in hand, for his afternoon jump with Stu. By the time the jump was finished, the propeller I'm holding was installed, and the engine run.

One time all summer Paul Hansen was the first one awake. He took this picture. Then he went back to sleep under the wing.

Aerobatics and dogfights over the fields brought people to watch the sky-gypsies, and to fly with them, $3 the ride.

Anybody who likes to get down from the sky the way Stu does is not only out of his mind, but a valuable member of any flying circus.

After supper, we carried lots of passengers. But during the day . . .

Stu and I in Palmyra, Wisconsin. Except for the shape of its automobiles, Midwest America hasn't changed much from the days of the first barnstormers.

Paul's first attempt at flying the biplane was not exactly what we could call an unqualified success.

A few turns. Give the passengers a feeling of flight.

Midnight thunderstorms can smash windows, but a gypsy pilot and his plane discover, somehow, a way to survive.

years old, with a barnstormer in a two-winger airplane, just like this one. "My boss told me you were here and I better not miss it."

A young fellow with a fantastic mop of a haircut stopped and looked at the airplane for a long time before he decided to fly. As Stu fastened him into the front seat he said, "Will I see tomorrow?"

This was pretty strange sentence structure, coming from a fellow who proclaimed himself illiterate. (For shame, I thought, judging the man by his haircut!) In flight, he braced hard against the turns, fearful, and after we landed he said, "*Wow!*" He stayed for a long time after his ride, looking at the airplane almost in awe. I put him down as a real person, in spite of the haircut. Something about being above the ground had reached through to him.

A pair of pretty young ladies in kerchiefs put our account-book in the black for the day, and they laughed happy in the sky, turning over their home town.

I checked the fuel, and with ten gallons left I was at the end of my margin, and it was time to fill the tank even though passengers had to wait.

I took off at once for the airport that Ev had mentioned, and in five minutes was rolling to a stop by the gas pump. I was just topping the tank when a burly, bright-eyed business-man in a snap-brim straw hat brisked out to the airplane.

"Hey, Dick!"

"CARL LIND!" He was just as I remembered him, one of the happiest people in the world. He had survived a heart at-tack, and now enjoyed the very air he breathed.

He looked the airplane over with an appraising eye. "Is it good, Carl?" I said. "Is it the way you remember?"

"We didn't have all that flashy gold paint, in my day, I can tell you. But the skid's pretty nice, and the patches in the wings. That's how I remember it."

"Hop in, Carl, get in the front here, if you trust me. You got no controls in front. I'm goin' back over to the field."

"Are you going to let me go along? Are you sure I can go?"

"Get in or you make us late. We got passengers waiting!"

"Never let 'em wait," he said, and stepped up into the front seat. We were airborne in less than a minute and it was good to see the man again in the sky he loved. He took off his hat, his gray hair blew in the wind, and he smiled hugely, remembering.

The biplane gave him a gentle landing in the hay, and I left the engine running while Carl stepped down.

"You go ahead and fly your passengers," he said. "Then we'll cover the airplane up and you come on over to the house."

We flew riders steadily till the sun was below the horizon, and all the time Carl Lind watched the biplane fly, waiting with his wife, and with Ev. It was the best weekday yet; twenty passengers by sundown.

"I don't know if this is in the Barnstormer's Code," I said to Carl as we drove around the edge of Lake Geneva and wound among the estates there. "We're supposed to get all dirty and always stay under the wing when we're not flying."

"Oh, no. They used to do this. Someone who liked airplanes would take you home for dinner."

But not, I thought as we turned into his drive, in quite this manner. It was a scene clipped from a Fine House magazine, all in full color and with deep carpets and full-length glass facing the water.

"This is our little place . . ." Carl began, apologetically.

Stu and I laughed at the same time. "Just a little shack you keep out in the woods, Carl?"

"Well . . . you like to have a place you can come and relax, you know?"

We got a brief tour of the elegant house, and it was a strange feeling. We felt close to something civilized. Carl enjoyed his house immensely, and it was a glad place, because of this.

"You fellows can change in here. We'll go down for a swim. You will. I'll catch two fish in the first five casts. Betcha, I will."

It was nearly full dark when we walked barefoot down the velvet sloping lawn to his dock. At one side of the white-painted wood was a boathouse, and an inboard speedboat hung there on winches.

"The battery's probably dead. But if we get it started, we'll go for a ride."

He lowered the boat into the water on its electric winch and pressed the starter. There was only a hollow clank and silence.

"I've got to remember to keep that battery up," he said, and hoisted the boat back into the air.

Carl had brought a little fishing pole with him and he began working for his Two Fish in the First Five Casts just at the moment that Stu and I hit the water in running dives off the dock. The lake was clear dark black, like pure oil that had been aged twenty years in ice. We swam furiously out to the light-float a hundred feet offshore and from there we watched the last sun fade from the sky. As it disappeared, so did every single sound in the Midwest, and a whisper from our float carried easily to shore.

"Carl, you've got a pretty rugged life," I said, from way out in the water.

"Two more years and then I'm going to retire. Quicker than that, if I get all this business done on my flying medical. Why, if I could fly alone, I'd retire this year! But if I can't fly, and just had to stay around here, it would get pretty bad."

He caught a fish on his second cast, and let it fall back into the dark water.

We cast off from the buoy and swam slowly to the dock. The wooden ladder-rungs were smooth and soft in moss, and when we stood again on the white planks, the air was warm as summer night.

"I lose my bet," Carl said. "All your splashing scared my fish away. Five casts and only one fish."

By the time we had returned to the house and changed into our least-greasy clothes, Everett had gone and come again, setting a huge steaming bag on the table. "I got twelve hamburgers," he said. "That ought to be enough, don't you think? And a gallon of root beer."

We sat that evening around a table by the fireplace in Carl's glass-walled den, eating hamburgers.

"I had to sell the Bird, you know," Carl said.

"What? Why? That was your *airplane!*"

"Yes, sir. But I couldn't stand it. Going out there and washing her down and waxing her, and not being able to fly by myself; this medical thing, you know. It wasn't right for the airplane, it wasn't right for me. So I sold her. Thelma still has her Cessna, and we go places now and then." He finished his hamburger. "Hey, I have something I want you to see." He left the table and went into the living room.

"I do hope that medical paper comes through," Thelma Lind said. "It means a lot to Carl."

I nodded, thinking it unjust that a man's life be so much affected by what to all the rest of the world was only a scrap of paper. If I were Carl, I'd burn all the paper in the fireplace and go out and fly my airplane.

"Here's something you'll love to see," Carl said, returning.

He unrolled a long photograph on the table and we looked down at a row of ten biplanes parked in front of a hangar.

White-ink letters at the lower right corner said *June 9, 1929*.

"These are the boys I used to fly with. Look at those guys. What do you think of that?"

He named each one of the pilots, and they looked out at us proud and unfaded, arms folded, standing by their airplanes. There at one side stood a young Carl Lind, in white collar and tie and knickers, not yet president of Lind Plastic Products, not yet concerned about a medical certificate. He wouldn't be thinking about that for another thirty-five years.

"Look here, huh? Long-Wing Eaglerock, Waco Ten, Canuck, Pheasant . . . now there's some real airplanes, don't you think? We used to go out to the Firemen's Picnic . . ."

It was a good evening, and I was glad that my years had overlapped Carl's. He had been flying and smiling up out of that photograph seven years before I was born.

"Be glad for your friends," Carl said. "We know people, don't we, Thelma, with millions of dollars, but without one friend in the world. Boys, be glad for your friends." He was deadly sincere, and to break the gravity of the moment he smiled at Stu. "You having fun out here in the cow-pastures, flying around?"

"I'm having more continuous fun than I've ever had in my life," the kid said, and just about startled me off my chair. He hadn't said such a revealing thing all summer long.

It was midnight when we zipped ourselves into our hot sleeping bags and settled down under the wing of the biplane.

"It's a tough life, isn't it, Stu?"

"Yep. Mansions, chocolate cake, swimming in Lake Geneva . . . this barnstorming is rough!"

A farmer was out by the huge Gothic cow-barn across the way at six a.m. He was a tiny dot by the base of the barn, dwarfed by the tremendous double-sloped roof with its four giant ventilators lined along the rooftrees seventy feet in the air. He was a quarter-mile away, but his voice came clear across the calm morning hay.

"BIDE BIDE BIDE BIDE BIDE! HURRY IT UP, BOSSY! C'MON C'MON C'MON!"

I woke and lay under the wing in the early light, trying to figure out what "Bide" meant. And "Bossy." Do farmers still call their cows "Bossy"? But there was the call again, coming across the fragrance of the hay, making me feel guilty to be lying abed when there were cows to be gotten out.

A dog barked, and day began in America.

I reached for pen and paper, to remind me to ask about BIDE, and as I wrote, a tiny six-legged creature, smaller than my pen-point, came hiking across the blue-lined page. I added, "A very small pointy-nosed bug just walked across this page—purposefully, definitely going somewhere _____⟶. He stopped here."

Were we, also, hiking along some cosmic journal-page? Were the events about us all part of a message we could understand, if only we found the right perspective from which to read them? Somehow, with our long series of miracles, of which this field at Walworth was the latest, I thought so.

Our morning check of the biplane showed that we had come up against our first problem of maintenance. The tail-skid was wearing thin. At one time it had a steel roller and metal plate to guard it, but the constant takeoffs and landings had worn those away. If we had to, we could whittle another skid from a tree-branch, but this was the time for preventive work. We talked about it on the way in for breakfast, and decided to look around the hardware store.

Close as it was to the resortlands of Lake Geneva, Walworth was becoming a very modern small town, and we found Hardware in the shopping center.

"May I help you?" the clerk said.

"Well, yes," I said, slowly and carefully. "We are looking for a tail skid shoe. Would you have anything in that line?"

How strange it was. If one doesn't stay well within the bounds of what one is expected to say, his words might as well be Swahili.

"Beg pardon?"

"A tail . . . skid . . . shoe. Our tail skid is wearing out."

"I don't think . . . a what?"

"We'll browse around, thanks."

We walked the rows of hardware, looking for a long narrow strip of metal, with holes for screws to mount it on the wooden skid. There were some big hinges that might work, a mason's trowel, a big heavy end wrench.

"Here we go," Stu said, from across the room. He held a tail skid shoe. The label on it said *Vaughn Spring Steel Super Bar*. It was a small flat crowbar that had clearly been made by a tail-skid-shoe company.

"Oh, you mean a pry-bar!" the clerk said. "I wasn't sure what you were looking for."

The room where we had breakfast had been in town somewhat longer than the shopping center. The only thing that had changed since saloon days was they had replaced the batwing doors, turned the furniture into museum pieces, and mounted lifelike detail drawings of *"Hamburger," "Cheeseburger,"* and *"French Fries"* in wide glowing plastic cases over the mirror, and over at least a thousand glasses stacked upside down.

Hanging on the wall was a rough old triangle of oak, notched like a great blunt saw along one edge, and bolted to some other moving sections of wood. *"Wagon Jack"* was printed on a board a few inches beneath it.

"Stu."

"Yeah."

"The tail of the Parks weighs more than all the rest of the

airplane put together. We've got to lift it to put on our new skid shoe."

"We'll lift it."

"Do you figure we could maybe borrow that wagon jack over there, somehow, and use it?"

"That's an antique wagon jack," he said. "They'd never loan it out to pick up an airplane."

"Won't hurt to ask. But how do we make it work?"

We looked at the Jack, and it was dead quiet in our booth. There was no possible way that the Jack could have lifted anything. We couldn't imagine how it might have picked up any wagon ever built. We sketched all over the backs of napkins and placemats, drawing little wagons and the way that the oaken triangle might have done its work. At last Stu thought he understood, and tried to explain it to me, but it didn't make any sense. We didn't bother to ask about borrowing the Wagon Jack, and paid our bill mystified by that thing hanging on the wall.

"We could start the engine," I said, "and pick up the tail with the propblast. 'Course it might get a little windy while you sit back under the tail and put the thing on. About a hundred miles an hour, the wind."

"While *I* sit back there?"

We'd find some way to do it, I was sure.

Stu's thought wandered from the immediate problem. "How about flour?" he said. "Should I try flour? Take a bag of flour and cut it open just before I jump, and leave a trail coming down?"

"Give it a try."

So The Great American invested in 59 cents' worth of King's Ransom Pre-Sifted Flour. It was five cents cheaper than any other brand, is why we bought it.

The answer to the problem of holding the tail in the air

was solved as soon as we returned to the biplane. It was simple.

"Just take a couple of those oil cans, Stu, that we haven't opened yet. I'll pick up the tail good as I can and you set those cans under the rudder post to hold it up. OK?"

"Are you putting me on? That big heavy tail on these cans of OIL? There'll be oil all over the place!"

"A college man, and he says a thing like that. Have you never learned the Incompressibility of Fluids? I shall lecture upon that subject, if you wish. Or if you would rather, Mister MacPherson, you can just get down under the tail and stick those cans under the rudder post."

"OK, professor. Ready when you are."

With agonizing tremendous great effort, I lifted the tail a foot in the air for three full seconds, and Stu set the cans in place. They held, and I was as surprised as he was that they did.

"Now if you would like the mathematical details, Mister MacPherson, we can discuss them at length . . ."

The skid shoe was in place in ten minutes.

We stretched out under the wing to put Method C to the test, and sure enough, two cars stopped at the roadside before we were half asleep. Our passengers were girls on vacation from college, and they were goggle-eyed at the biplane.

"You mean it *flies*? Up in the *air*?"

"Yes ma'am. Guaranteed to fly. Look down on all the world. Three dollars a ride and a prettier day we couldn't ask, could we?"

Jouncing out to the far end of the hayfield, and as we turned into the wind to begin the flight, my riders were overcome by second thoughts. They shouted quickly to each other, over the noise of the engine and the rattling of the hollow-drum flying machine. About the time they had decided that they had been out of their *minds* to even *think* of going up in this *old dirty machine,* the throttle came forward, they were engulfed in the great twisting roar of the engine, and we were clatterbanging over the hard ground, hurtling toward the highway and the cars and the telephone wires. They clutched the soft leather rim of the front cockpit and at the moment we left the ground they gasped and looked and held even tighter. Someone screamed. The wires flashed below and we climbed easily up into the sky.

They turned to look back at the ground and at me, quizzically. The realization swept over them that this madman sitting in the cockpit behind them now held the key to their entire future. He looked unshaven. He looked as if he didn't have much money. Could he be trusted?

I smiled in what I hoped was a disarming way, and pointed to the lake. They turned to look at the table-napkin sailboats and the cut-glass sparkle of sun on the water, and I went back to picking my forced-landing fields, turning ever so slightly so that we would never be out of gliding range from them.

It was fun to see what a different pilot I became for my different passengers. I had flown a few folk who had left mink jackets in their Cadillac convertibles, and for these few I was a two-dimensional creature, a blank-faced chauffeur, taking this flying all as a very boring job and unaware that the lake from the air was even mildly attractive. A hired man cannot be expected to appreciate the finer things. These people got a straight conventional ride, a ride that they would get from an uninspired workhorse chauffeur. Take off. Circle town. Circle lakeshore. Circle town. Land. Everything by the book.

The college girls, all windblown ahead of me now, had taken the biplane for something of a gay novelty, and for them I was a gay novelty of a pilot, with a bright disarming smile. For them, I could know that flying can be pretty, I could even point a good place to look. One of the girls looked back at me with a how-pretty-it-is glance, and I smiled again, to say that I understood.

Most of the passengers flew just for the fun and adventure of the flight, and with them I made experiments. I found that I could make most people look where I wanted them to look; it was just a matter of banking the airplane in that direction.

I could test their aptitude for flying, too, by banking. When a person sits up straight in the seat, riding with the airplane through the turns, when he looks fearless down to the ground during a steep bank, when he doesn't bother to grip the cockpit rim, he is a natural born airplane pilot. About one passenger in sixty met the tests, and I always made it a point to tell them of the fact . . . that if they ever wanted to fly an airplane, they would be very good pilots. Most just shrugged and said it was fun. I felt sad, knowing that I couldn't have passed those tests myself, before I began to fly.

For the girls, now, as I steepened the bank, the biplane was a noisy high carnival ride. At 40 degrees of bank, the girl on the right screamed and hid her eyes. When we leveled, she looked out again, and again we would gradually increase the bank. Every time, when we tilted to precisely 40 degrees, she would make some kind of cry and bury her face in her hands. At 39 degrees she looked down happy; at 40, she screamed. Her friend looked back at me and shook her head, smiling.

On the last turn before landing, the turn closest to the ground and with the most sense of speed and blurred action, we banked up to 70 degrees and fell like a cannonball toward the ground. The girl on the right didn't uncover her eyes until we were stopped again next to her car.

I shut the engine down while Stu helped them from the cockpit.

"Oh it's WONDERFUL! It's just *WONDERFUL!*" she said.

Her companion thanked us quietly, but the other girl couldn't get over how wonderful it was. I shrugged. The wonderfullest parts to me were the parts that she had closed her eyes upon.

They left, waving, and in a few minutes Method C brought Everett Feltham back to us, with a box of rags.

"Hey, you sack rats! Why don't you come on out to the house and eat up some strawberries, huh?"

It took us three minutes to tie the covers on the airplane and find a place in his car. We spent the next hours with Ev, fetching a case of oil for the biplane and sitting in the shade of his elms, consuming great bowls of strawberries and vanilla ice cream.

"Man, this barnstorming is rugged, Ev," I said, leaning back in my lawn chair. "You don't ever want to try it."

"I'll bet. You guys sure look overworked, lyin' down under that wing out there. I wish I had a biplane. Be with you in a flash."

"OK. Get a biplane. Join The Great American. Any other problems?"

Ev had a schedule to fly out of O'Hare International that afternoon, so dropped us off on his way toward Chicago. We said those goodbyes that flyers say, a confident sort of "See-you-'round," certain that they actually will, as long as they don't make any very dumb mistakes while handling their airplanes.

Stu dragged out his parachute, still field-packed from his last jump, and stretched it out on the ground for final packing. A pair of boys arrived to watch and ask questions about what it feels like to fall all alone through the air, and what the parts of the chute were called and where you learn to jump.

"Gonna jump today?" one said. "Pretty soon, maybe?"

"Not if the wind comes up much more."

"Gee, it isn't windy."

"It is if you're coming down in this thing." He worked on in silence.

An airplane flew up from the south, circled town, then swung down low over our field. It was Paul Hansen in the Luscombe, flashing overhead at 120 miles per hour, pulling up steep into the blue, swinging back down for another pass. We waved to him.

The Luscombe flew across the field three times, measuring it. I put myself in his cockpit, looking down at the hayfield, flying the heavy-laden sportplane. I squinted my eyes and finally shook my head. I wouldn't do it; I wouldn't land. The field was right for the biplane, but the biplane had more than twice the wing area of the Luscombe. The field was too short for Paul's airplane; he could make it, but just barely, with no margin over the telephone wires. If he landed here, I would make a big thing of how unwise he was.

On the fourth pass, he kicked the rudder back and forth to signal "No," and flew out to the airport down the road.

The problems of working with a single-wing airplane, I thought. He needs just too much runway. And this is a good field, right in close to town, that saved us when we were broke, and that has lots of passengers yet to fly.

I pulled the covers off the Parks and made her ready to go. Darn. A good hayfield . . .

When I landed at the airport, Paul was tying down his airplane. He was still wearing his white shirt and tie.

"Halloo," I said. " 'D you get your pictures all took?"

"Yeah. Made it in here nonstop from Ohio, that's why I didn't stay any longer over the field there. Just about out of gas. And that field is too short for me." He was apologetic, as if it was his fault that the field wasn't right.

"No prob. Throw your stuff in the front seat and we'll hop on over. If you trust me. No controls up front . . ."

It took a while for the 1960's to fade from Paul, and as he helped Stu finish packing the chute, he told us about the shootings he had done. It was depressing to hear that the other world still existed, out there, with people still running around in business suits and discussing abstracts that had nothing to do with engines or tailskids or good fields to land in.

That evening, even without a parachute jump, the biplane had fifteen passengers to carry, and when she was covered for the night, we were sure again that an unorganized barn-stormer could get along in spite of a few lean days.

There was the usual lively conversation over the restaurant table, but all the while, in the back of my mind, I was thinking about the Luscombe unable to work the short fields. If it had been hard to find this place where the biplane could land, it was going to be twice as hard to find a hayfield long enough for both airplanes to work well.

A barnstormer can survive, but is he stacking the cards against himself by working with an airplane that wasn't built for short-field flying? Would the Luscombe be the downfall of The Great American and its dreams? I couldn't get the questions out of my mind.

CHAPTER TWELVE

I CHECKED THE TAILSKID SHOE first thing in the morning. It needed some extra wire to hold it in place and this meant lifting the tail back onto the oil cans.

Paul stood glumly by.

"Think you could give me a hand with lifting the tail?" I said. "Stu, you ready for us to lift?"

"Lift away," said Stu from his oilcans underneath the tail.

Paul apparently hadn't heard me, for he didn't move to help. "Hey, Paul! Why don't you stop sucking that cigarette for a minute and give us a hand here?"

Paul looked at me as though I was some kind of repugnant beetle, and moved to help. "All right, all right I'll help you! Take it easy."

We picked up the tail and set the skid on its oilcan jack. Later, we walked to town for breakfast and Paul trailed behind, saying nothing, the picture of depression. Whatever his problem is, I thought, it is none of my business. If he wants to be depressed, that's his option. It was the quietest, most uncomfortable breakfast we ever had. Stu and I traded comments about the weather and the tail skid and the wagon jack, how it couldn't possibly work, and all the time Paul said not a word, made no sound at all.

We all had separate places to go after breakfast, and for the first time since we began the summer, we did not walk together, but went three separate ways. It was an interesting sort of thing, but puzzling, for the same wave of depression hit us all.

Well, heck, I thought, walking alone back to the airplane, I don't care. If the other guys want to do something else and feel bad, I can't stop 'em. The only guy I can control is me, and I'm out here to barnstorm, not to waste time feeling bad.

I resolved to fly to the airport and change the biplane's oil, and then I was pushing on. If the other guys wanted to come along, that was fine with me.

When I walked onto the hayfield again, Paul was sitting alone on his sleeping bag, writing a note. He said nothing.

"OK, buddy," I said at last. "What you do is none of my business except when it starts to affect me. And it's starting. What is bugging you?"

Paul stopped writing, and folded the paper. "You," he said. "Your attitude has changed. You've been acting different ever since I got back. I'm leaving today. I'm on my way home."

So that was the problem. "You're free to go. You mind telling me just how my attitude has changed? I no longer want to fly with you, is that it, you guess?"

"I don't know. But you're just not there. I might as well be some brand new guy you never met before. You can treat other people like outsiders, but you can't treat me that way."

I scanned back over everything I had done or said since Paul returned. I had been a trifle stiff and formal, but I had been that way a thousand times since I had known Paul. I am stiff and formal with my airplane when we haven't flown for a few days. It must have been my comment about the cigarette this morning. Even as I had said it, it sounded a bit harsher than it was meant to be.

"OK," I said. "I apologize. I'm sorry for my crack about the cigarette. I keep forgetting you're so darn sensitive . . ."

Heck of an apology, I thought.

"No, it's not that only. It's your whole attitude. It's like you can't wait to get rid of me. So don't worry. I'm getting out. I was writing a note to leave for you, but you came back too quick to finish it."

I stood there. Had I been so wrong for so long? Would this man, whom I considered among the very best friends I had in the world, judge me without listening for my defense, find me guilty and then leave without a word?

"The only thing I can think of . . ." I started slowly, trying to speak as truly as I could, ". . . is that I wish to goodness you would have been able to land in this field. I was mad at you when you didn't land, because this is such a good field. But I wouldn't land the Luscombe here myself, and I think you'd be dumb to try it. You did the right thing, but I just wished that the Lusk could be a little better barnstorming airplane, is all." I began to roll my sleeping bag. "If you want to bug out, fine. But if you leave because you think I want to get rid of you, you're wrong, and that's your problem to overcome."

We talked the trouble back and forth, and gradually we were talking like ourselves again, bridging a chasm that had been hidden under ice.

"Are you going to settle down now," Paul said, "and treat your troops like they were human beings?"

"All this time I thought we had forgot about who was leader," I said, "and you been thinking I was the honcho. I resign, I tell you, I resign!"

Airborne, flying again as barnstormers in formation, we searched to the north first, without results. The land close to the towns was everywhere too rough and too short for both airplanes. I looked down again at the broad grass strip at Lake Lawn and thought that we could be an interesting diversion for the golfers, and probably make much money. But golfers were urban people, living way out ahead of us in time, concerned about unreal things . . . profit margins and credit ratings and the life of giant cities. We were looking to fly with the people of the world to which our airplanes belonged.

We followed the road west and south, and again crossed down into the heat of summer Illinois. We circled eight or ten little towns, left the road for a river, and finally rolled our wheels in the grass of an airstrip by the river. It was a good long strip. There was plenty of room for the Luscombe to work fully loaded, and we were one mile from a town. A little far out, but worth trying.

The field was surrounded by oats and corn, set low in the wide long valley of the river. There was a farmhouse at the end of the strip, and a small hangar.

Two minutes after we landed, a light twin-engine airplane touched down and taxied near the hangar.

"Sure," the owner said. "You boys can work out of here if you want. Be nice to get some folks out to the airport."

We were working again. Our first acquaintance with Pecatonica, Illinois, was a friendly one.

In long sheds near the farmhouse were a great number of pigs, snarkling and gorkling as we found that pigs are wont to do. A man and his wife came from the house to wonder who we were, shyly followed by a little girl who peeked around her mother's skirts. The girl was stricken silent in awe. She was convinced that we were Martians landing in some strange sort of saucers, and goggled at us, set to dash screaming into the house at the first monster-word we said. Stu walked down the lane to post our signs, and the girl kept an eye on him, lest he creep up behind and devour her in one toothy gnash.

There were two hundred pigs in the shed, we learned, and wandering around somewhere were nine cats and a horse. The horse, at the moment, was kept in a grassy lot, and trotted over to talk with us when we walked near his gate.

"This is Skeeter," the woman said. "Raised him from a colt. Skeeter is a wonderful horse . . . aren't you, Skeeter?" She rubbed his velvet nose.

Skeeter made some comment, a low polite whinny, and nodded his head. He left us then, trotted once around the perimeter of his grass and came back to lift his head sociably over the gate. Skeeter had a very outgoing personality.

"Goin' toward town . . . you boys want a lift?" the owner said. We did, and jumped into the back of a red pickup. As we turned down the lane and onto the highway, it was Paul who asked the question.

"How do you think it's going to go?"

"Looks OK," Stu said.

"Little far out, maybe," I said, "but we'll do all right."

Pecatonica's main street was high-curbed and lined with glass store fronts and wood facades. The center of town was one block long: hardware, cafés, the Wayne Feed Dealer, service station, dime store. We hopped down from the truck at the beginning of the block, called our thanks and walked to a café for lemonade.

It was full hot summer, with the round plastic advertising thermometers pointing 95 degrees. We ordered giant lemonades and looked at the ceiling and walls. It was the same long narrow room we had come to expect, with booths down one wall, and the counter and mirror and stacked glasses down the other, kitchen way at the back with a round order-wheel hanging from its pivot in the pass-through window. The ceiling was at least 15 feet high, tiled in green floral-stamped tin.

It was all a clever electrical museum out of 1929, with ani-
mated people who could move and talk and blink their eyes.

Our waitress was a startlingly pretty girl who smiled as she
brought our lemonade. She didn't seem at all electrical.

"Are you going to come out and fly with us?" Paul asked.

"Oh! You're the boys with the airplanes! I saw you fly over
a little while ago. Two of you?"

"And a jumper," I added.

It was beyond understanding. We had made only a half-
circle of town, but surely half the people in Pecatonica knew
about the two airplanes waiting at the airport.

We piled our lemonade money on the table.

"You'll be out to fly with us?" Paul said.

"I don't know. I might."

"She won't," Paul said. "Why is it that waitresses never
come out and fly with us?"

"Waitresses are the best judges of character in the world,"
I told him. "They know never to fly with people who wear
nutty green hats."

Taking our lemonade with us, we set out for the airport.
It was a fifteen-minute walk, and by the time we reached the
strip we were thirsty again. In the shed next to the pigs' home
there were several tractors and some bales of hay for Skeeter.
The children were out in the yard, and no sooner had Stu
laid himself down on the hay than they ran over and began
burying him in kittens. There was a mother cat with them,
and while Paul and I chatted with Skeeter, Stu was flat on his
back in the hay, being trampled by a child-directed stampede
of kittens. He was enjoying it greatly, and I was surprised.
Stu was stepping out of character; this was not the sort of
thing I had come to expect from our thoughtful, taciturn
jumper.

Paul and I soon had the airplanes fired up and we flew one
brief dogfight over the edge of town. There were four cars

waiting when we landed, and a few passengers. We went to work flying.

At last I got a thumbs-down signal from Stu that there were no passengers waiting, and shut down the Whirlwind.

Paul had just come down, and his passenger, an attractive young lady of nineteen or twenty, in a rather low-cut summer dress, walked directly to me.

"Hello," she said, "My name is Emily."

"Hi, Emily."

"I just got down from my very first airplane ride and it's just wonderful! Everything's so pretty! But Paul said that if I *really* wanted to have fun, I should ride with you!"

Paul thought I was off-balance whenever confronted by a pretty woman, and Emily could only be a part of his experimenting to prove it. I glanced at the Luscombe, and there was Paul, all right, polishing spots from his spotless engine cowl, all of a sudden looking very intently at his work.

I'd show him. "Why Emily, ol' Paul was 'zackly right. You want to know what flying really is, you just pop right over to that young fella there in the yellow jumpsuit and get yourself a ticket, and we'll go flying."

She looked downcast for a moment, and moved to stand very close to me. "I'm all out of money, Dick," she said softly.

"I don't believe it! Three dollars is nothin' for a ride in a biplane! Not many left, nowadays, you know."

"I'd sure love to fly with you," she cooed.

"Be worth it, too, ma'm. A beautiful day to fly. Well—as you know, if you were just up with Paul."

She was in no hurry to rush off and pay Stu her three dollars and was happy just to stand and talk and let the sun reflect bright colors from her low summer dress.

Just then an earlier passenger was back, wanting another "wild ride." I said a careful goodbye to the girl, started the Wright and taxied out. As I passed the Luscombe, I shook my head slowly at Paul, who was now quite vigorously polishing the propeller. We never saw Emily again.

The morning roadside on the walk back from breakfast was deep in purple flower.

"Hey, you guys," I said, "Honey-clover!"

"Pretty."

"No, it's not pretty, it's good to eat. Like when you were a kid, remember?" I picked a boll and tasted the hollow petals. There was a tenth of a drop of nectar in each one, a delicate sweet flavor of morning. Paul and Stu tried one each, as we walked.

"Tastes like eating a flower," Stu said.

"Can't figure you guys out." I picked another handful of purple, and crunched on the tender petals. "This great stuff growin' all over, and you walk right by."

There was a concrete bridge between town and the airport, crossing the one straightest mile on the length of the Pecatonica River. We heard the sound of outboard motors, and a pair of tiny racing hydroplanes came buzzing full throttle down the river, battling for the lead. They roared echoing under the bridge and through in an instant. The drivers wore helmets and heavy lifejackets, and they were completely absorbed in their race. At the end of the straight they slowed, turned and came back again, tall arcs of spray leaping behind them. It was a sort of aquatic Dragging Main, but somehow it seemed a much cleaner sport.

We walked on across the bridge, and past a lawn where a boy was beating a rug with a twisted wire hoop.

"What's the plan?" Paul said as we walked by Skeeter, who whinnied, and out to the airplanes. "You want to try for something during the day again? Might get somebody."

"Anything you say."

"I'm running out of time," Paul said. "I should head back

pretty soon. Take me three days to get home from here, about."

"Well, let's give it a try; go up and fly a bit," I said. "Might get a couple people out to fly. Be cool, anyway."

We took off and climbed to 3,000 feet in formation over the summer town. The hydroplanes hadn't stopped; their twin white wakes still ran neck-and-neck along the dark river. The boy was still beating the rug half a mile beneath us and I shook my head. It had been 20 minutes since we walked by. What a devoted young fellow that must be, beating a rug for 20 minutes. Three minutes of rug-beating used to be my outside limit. The world is an earnest place, in 1929.

Paul broke away in a wide sweeping turn and swung around toward me to begin the old familiar aerial battle. I pulled the biplane's nose straight up in the air, hoping for the Luscombe to swish right on by beneath me and give me the chance of dropping down on her tail. The first part of our dogfights were never staged; we were trying our best to work into a firing position behind each other. It was only at the end that I had to let Paul win, because I had the smoke flare and was still the only one eligible to go down in flames.

The earth twisted around us in green, sky in blue, and for a while I didn't care whether potential passengers were watching or not. It would not do, in this first part of our game, to let Paul get behind the biplane. I had Air Force training in this business long before he learned to fly; I had practiced air combat in front-line military fighters while Paul was still taking fashion pictures in his elegant studio.

Everyone else I knew began to fly in slow airplanes, little airplanes, old airplanes, and then went with the times. In a few years they were flying faster, bigger, more modern machines. It had been just the other way around for me.

First had come the seamless military trainers and fighters and air combat at transsonic speed, then the transports, then modern businessplanes, then an aging lightplane, now this biplane locked firmly into the day before yesterday. From airborne weapons radar to modern electronics to a simple panel of radio to nothing at all—the biplane was not only without radio, she was entirely without electricity. She was back in the days when a pilot was his own man, with no links to ground-people to aid him or to annoy him. 1929 is a happy year, but sometimes, watching a contrail pulling along way up in the stratosphere, I had to admit to myself that I missed the power and speed and the high lonesome joy of the fighter pilot. Sometimes.

The Luscombe was beside me now, trying desperately to slow down, to fall behind the biplane's tail. I pushed full throttle, held the nose up, looked across the air at Paul, and laughed. The little sportplane could stand it no longer; all at once it shuddered and fell away toward the ground, stalled out. I pressed full rudder as the Parks stalled a second later and dropped down on the Luscombe's tail. My reputation was secure. No matter what happened now, I could tell Paul that I deliberately gave him the advantage, after once having been on his tail. He pulled up again, rolling inverted, dropped away, spinning the sky around us both as I rolled to follow.

Stu was already at work convincing the customers it was a great day for flying, and by noon we had flown five passengers. We spent the afternoon in the shade of the wings, trying to stay cool. It wasn't an easy job.

A few minutes after I had finally made it into sleep, Paul came over and woke me up. "What do you say to some watermelon? Wouldn't that be great? Nice cold watermelon?"

"Sounds keen. You go in and get it and I'll help eat."

"No, c'mon. Let's go get a watermelon."

"You're out of your mind. It's a mile to town!"

"Stu! How about going in and us getting a watermelon?"

Paul said. "Then we could bring it out here and eat it and not give Bach any."

"You go in and get it," Stu said. "I'll wait here for you."

"Aw. I just can't wait around here doing nothing. I'm going to go up and do some flip-flops."

"Fine," I said. Stu was already asleep.

Paul took off a few minutes later and I watched some of his flying. Then I turned over and found a cooler place under the wing.

I didn't hear him taxi in and stop, but he woke us again. "Hey, we have to get some watermelon. Nobody's coming out to fly."

"Tell you what, Paul," I said. "You go in and get the watermelon, and I'll let you use my knife to cut it. How's that sound?"

A few minutes later a truck pulled out from the hangar, headed for town, and Paul was aboard. He had a fixation about that watermelon. Well, I thought as I went back to sleep, if he wants a watermelon that much, he should get his watermelon.

Half an hour later we heard Skeeter whinny hello and Paul was back, a watermelon under his arm. It was 100 degrees in the sun and he had lugged the thing all the way from town.

"Hey you guys," he called. "Watermelon!"

It was hard to understand, I thought, munching on the cool goodness. If I was Paul, I would have let the lazy louts starve out there under the wing. At most, I might have thrown them a bit of rind. But share the first part of my watermelon with them? Never!

"I guess I better bug on out," Paul said. "We're not going to have many passengers, at least till late. It's a long way back to California, and I might as well get started on it today." He began separating his belongings from the pile of equipment, and set them neatly into his airplane. Cameras, film cases, bedroll, clothes bag, maps. "I'll leave you guys the watermelon," he said.

A car drove into the lane, and another.

"We have discovered a delayed-action Method C," I said as a third car parked across the grass.

We started the Parks and Stu went over to talk to the people. First passengers were a man and his boy, and the man wore a set of goggles he had last worn in the tank corps in Africa. They said a few wind-blasted words and we were airborne, climbing toward the river up to the cool high air.

"Hey, that's really nice," the man said, eleven minutes later, as Stu helped him out. "Really nice. You can really see a long way from up there, can't you?"

Stu closed the door after the next passengers and stopped by my cockpit. "You've got two first-timers and one's a little scared."

"OK." I wondered why he had said that. Most of our passengers were up for the first time, and most were a bit apprehensive, though they didn't often show it. These must be more worried than usual about flying in the rachety old biplane. But as soon as we were halfway through the first circle of town, they had relaxed and were asking for steep banks. It is the unknown that worries our passengers, I thought. As soon as they see what flying is like, and that it is even a little bit pretty, then it becomes known and nice, and there's no cause for fear. Fear is just a way of thinking, a feeling. Get rid of that feeling by knowing what is true in the world, and you aren't afraid.

Business was suddenly going strong. There were eight cars parked on the grass, and Stu was ready with two more passengers when I rolled to a stop.

Paul walked to my cockpit. "Looks like a thunderstorm

west. I'll be doing good to make Dubuque by dark," he said. "I'm pushing it, aren't I?"

"You're never pushing it as long as you can control your airplane, remember," I said. "If you don't like the looks of things, just go down and land in a field and wait it out. You might as well stay one more night here, don't you think, anyway?"

"Nope. Better be on my way, get back home. You've got four passengers waiting for you, no need me waiting around to say goodbye. I'll get right on out."

"OK, Paul. It's been fun."

Stu closed the door on the new passengers and waved that they were ready to go.

"Yeah. Been fun," Paul said. "We should run it again next year, huh? Maybe a little longer."

"OK. Take it easy. Fly good, and set down if the weather gives you a hard time."

"Yeah. Put me on your postcard list."

I nodded and pulled my goggles down, pushed the throttle forward. What a brusque goodbye, after flying together for so long.

We took off over the corn, and climbed up through the warm evening air, turning toward town, over the river. I saw the Luscombe airborne, turning my way. Paul fell into formation for a minute or so, to the delight of the passengers, each of whom aimed a camera and jotted the moment down on film.

What did it mean, that this man who had flown with us, who was part of the risks and joys and work and trials, of the understanding and misunderstanding of barnstorming, was now leaving?

Paul waved goodbye, kicked the Luscombe up into a sudden sharp breakaway and accelerated out into the west, where the sun was blocked by a giant thundercloud.

It meant, strangely enough, not that he was leaving at all, but that he was there. That if the time ever came for another test of freedom, another plan to prove that we don't have to live any way but the way we wish, it might not have to be a lonely time. How many others like him are left in the country? I couldn't tell if there were ten or a thousand. But I did know there was one.

"See you around, buddy," I said. No one heard but the wind.

❧ CHAPTER THIRTEEN ❧

THE THUNDERSTORM HIT US at five in the morning, and we woke to raindrops clattering on the wing.

"We are going to get wet," Stu observed calmly.

"Well, sir, yes. We can either stay under this wing or we can chicken out and run for the tractor shed."

We decided to chicken out, grabbed our sleeping bags and ran for the shed, pelted all the way by heavy drops. I settled down by a doorway in the shed, where I could watch both the storm and the windsock. The rain didn't worry me, but it would have been nice to know whether or not there would be any hail. It would have to be large and sharp hail, and coming straight down, before it could hurt the airplane. I took some comfort in the thought that hail that bad would also hurt the corn and oats, and that corn and oats were rarely damaged by hail.

The biplane didn't seem at all concerned by the storm, and after a while I moved my sleeping bag over into the steel bucket of a Case 300 skip-loader. The heavy steel ridges of that bucket, covered by two layers of sleeping bag, made a comfortable bed. The only shortcoming was the rather noisy nearness of the pigs, with their ork-orking and clanging their metal feed-lids every few seconds. If I were a manufacturer of feed bins for hogs, I thought, I would glue big rubber strips on those lids to deaden the sound. Every 20 seconds . . . *clang!* I didn't know how Skeeter could stand it.

The rain stopped in an hour and Stu walked over to look at the animals eating. In a few minutes he walked back and began gathering his equipment from the shed. "Now I know where they get the expression 'pushy pig,' " he said.

We had our breakfast at the other café, and looked over our Texaco road map for Eastern United States.

"I'm getting tired of all this north stuff," I said. "Let's swing down into southern Illinois or Iowa or Missouri. Not Illinois. I'm tired of Illinois."

"Whatever you want," said Stu. "We could try a jump here, see what happens. Yesterday was a good day. Haven't had a chance to try out that flour, yet."

Later, Stu stood bulky on the wingwalk, holding to the strut and looking down. His target was the center of the field, but the wind was blowing hard at altitude, and carried the drift indicator a half-mile east of the strip. I thought he might cancel the jump, but he stood on the wing and motioned corrections that would take him to his jump point. The first jump run was not where he wanted it, and to make it worse, a patch of clouds hid the runway. We swung around to try again.

With Stu on the wing, the airflow over the tail of the biplane was broken all out of smoothness . . . the horizontal stabilizer bucked and jumped painfully, and the control stick shuddered in the force of the roiled wind. It was always a tense time, with him there, but this was even worse, swinging slowly around to try another pass in high winds aloft and with the stabilizer blurred under the strain of that shattered airflow.

The cloud crept slowly from over the field and the pass

looked better to Stu. He waved me two degrees right, two more degrees right, and then slit the bag of King's Ransom Flour. It trailed overboard in a great tunnel of white, our own contrail there at 4,000 feet. Then he jumped, still trailing flour.

I cut the throttle, banked hard to keep him in sight, and followed him down. It would never be routine; I was already wishing that he would hurry up and pull the ripcord.

Stu was a missile, launched in reverse. He had been still and waiting on the wing, he had fired down, and now he was going through his own sonic barriers and high-Q pressures.

At last he stopped his turns and deltas, pulled the ripcord, and the canopy snapped out into the sky. It was a piece of cake. He tracked into the wind, centered over his grassy target, and came down dead center, falling and leaping up again at once to spill the canopy.

By the time I landed he was ready to hop aboard for the short ride in.

"Nice jump, Stu!"

"Best one yet. Went just like I wanted it to go."

There was a crowd waiting, and I settled down for a long run of flying. It didn't work out that way. Only five people felt like flying, although one man handed Stu a ten-dollar bill and said, "Can you give me this much a ride?" We spent 20 minutes out over the countryside, and he still didn't tire of looking down.

A farmer was last to ride that morning, and we flew over his house and lands, green and bright after the rain. He didn't look at his land as much as he reflected upon it; I could see the thought in his face. So this is my land, so that is where I've spent my life. Sure, there's fifty other places like it all around, but this is my land and it's every acre good.

We broke for lunch when there were no passengers left to

fly, and caught a ride to town with one young man who had flown and stayed to watch.

"I sure envy you guys," he said as we turned onto the highway. "Bet you see a lot of girls, flying around."

"Yep, we see a lot of girls, all right," I said.

"Boy. I'd like to join you. But I got a job that ties me down."

"Well, quit your job," I said, testing him. "Come on and join us!"

"I couldn't do that. Couldn't quit my job . . ." He had failed his test. Not even girls could lure him away from a job that tied him down.

When we returned from lunch, I saw that the biplane was getting a little greasy. I selected a rag and began wiping the silver cowl.

"Why don't you get the windshields, Stu? There's so much grease on 'em the poor people can hardly see out."

"Sure thing."

We talked as we worked, and decided to stay in Pecatonica the rest of the day, and leave early next morning.

I backed off and looked at the airplane, and I was pleased. She was much prettier. Stu wiped the top of the cowl, which wasn't necessary. But there was something about the rag that he was using . . .

"Stu? That rag IS MY T-SHIRT! THAT'S MY T-SHIRT YOU'RE USING!"

He opened his mouth in terror, and froze solid.

"It was with all the other rags," he choked. "And it looked so . . . raggy." He unfolded it, helplessly. It was no longer cloth, but a mass of gooey rocker-grease. "God knows I'm sorry," he said.

"Aw, heck. Go ahead and use it for a rag. It was only my T-shirt."

He debated for a moment, looked at the shirt, and went

back to wiping grease with it. "I thought something was funny," he said. "It was an awful clean rag."

Method C picked up some passengers that afternoon, and the first was the man and his wife who lived at the airstrip. "We've been watching you, and you look pretty safe, so we decided to take the plunge."

They enjoyed the plunge. We circled over their house on the strip before landing, and as we did a car drew up and a man got out and knocked on the door.

The woman smiled and pointed down at him, so her husband could see. Their caller waited patiently for the door to be answered, not thinking to look up in the sky for his friends, a thousand feet overhead.

We landed and the woman ran laughing to keep him from driving away from an empty house.

Then business died away, though there were still some people standing to look at the biplane. One lean gentleman walked up and looked in the cockpit after I shut the engine down. "You ever heard of Bert Snyder?" he said.

"Can't say as I have . . . who's Bert Snyder?"

"Used to be Bert Snyder Circus, in 1923. Used to come into this town for the county fair. He had a whole lot of airplanes, a whole lot of them. And I used to be the most envied kid in town. I'd go up in the front of one of them airplanes and throw handbills out, advertising, all over the place. He had quite a circus. This town would be so full of people come to see him and come to the fair you couldn't turn around . . . old Bert Snyder."

"Sounds like quite a guy."

"Sure was . . . quite a guy. And you know, these kids you fly, they'll remember this ride for the rest of their lives. Oh, they'll fly jets all over the world, but they'll tell their kids, 'I remember when I went up, summer of '66, it was, in an old open-cockpit . . .' "

Of course he was right; sure he was right. We weren't here just for ourselves, after all. In how many albums and scrapbooks had The Great American already found immortality? In how many thoughts and memories did our images sleep this moment? I suddenly felt the weight of history and eternity upon us all.

At that moment another car arrived; our friend the tank driver. He had brought his wife out to fly, and as soon as she stepped from the car, she began laughing.

"Is this . . . the *airplane* . . . you wanted me to fly?"

I did not see what was so funny about it all, but she was laughing so hard that I was forced to smile. Maybe it *would* look funny, to some people.

The woman could not control herself. She laughed until there were tears in her eyes; she leaned against the side of the fuselage, buried her face in her hands and laughed. It wasn't long before everyone was laughing; she made us a very happy group.

"I admire your courage," she said, choking on her words. After a long while she settled down and even said that she was ready to fly.

We flew around town, made our turns and came back in to land, and she was still smiling when she got out of the airplane. I could only hope that the reason for the smile had changed.

The sun dropped into low gold on the horizon, and there was a faint mist through the valley that caught the color and sprayed it across the countryside. We had a crowd of twenty people around us, but all had either flown or had no wish to fly.

They had no idea what they were missing; this would be a magnificent sunset from the air.

"Come along, folks," I said. "Sunsets for sale this evening! The Great American Flying Circus guarantees a minimum of two sunsets this evening, but only if you act now! Watch the sun go down here, then up in the sky to watch her go down once more! A sight you will never see again, as long as you live! Prettiest sunset all summer! It's a burnt-copper afternoon—right out of Beethoven's heart! Who's ready to step up there into the air with me?"

One lady, sitting in a car nearby, thought I was speaking all to her. Her words came clear in the soft air, louder than she meant. "I don't fly unless I have to."

I was angry, sad. The poor people had no idea; with their caution, they were passing up paradise! How do you convince them of good? I made one last appeal, then, meeting no response, started the engine and took off alone, just to fly and to see the land from the air.

It was more beautiful than I had promised. The haze topped out at less than a thousand feet, and from 2,000 feet the earth was a silent lake of gold, with a few brilliant emerald hilltops rising to be islands in the crystal air. The land was all a golden dream, where only good and beautiful lived, and it was spread out below us like a tale from Marco Polo, with the sky going deep-velvet black overhead. It was another planet, that Earth, one never seen by man, and the biplane and I held the splendor of it all to ourselves.

We started our first roll a mile in the air, and the biplane did not stop rolling and soaring and diving and singing strong in her wires until the ground was dark and the mist was gone and the gold had disappeared from the sky.

We whispered down into the grass and swung to park, shutting the engine into hot-ticking silence. I sat alone for a full minute, not wanting to talk to people or to hear them or to see them. I knew I'd never forget that flight, and I wanted a quiet moment to lay it carefully away in my thought, for I would be coming back here many times again, in the years ahead.

Someone said low, in the crowd, "He has the courage of ten men, to fly that old crate."

I felt like crying. They didn't understand . . . I . . . could . . . not make . . . them . . . understand.

Gradually the cars drove away and the ground went very dark indeed. The hills on the horizon were powder-black against the last light of the sun; they stood with their trees and windmills and rolling fields in razor silhouette, like the skyline in a planetarium, just as the stars are being flashed upon the dome. Sharp and black and clear.

The old timer was the last one left, and as he slid into his car to leave, he said, "Young fella, how much would you say that airplane's worth, about?"

"Mister, if Henry Ford were to walk up here and want this machine, I'd tell him, 'Hank, you ain't got enough money to buy that airplane.'"

"I believe you'd say that," the man said, "I really believe you'd say that."

We counted our money over breakfast. We had flown twenty-eight passengers, and we showed a handsome profit.

"You know, Stu, with the little fields like this, the little airstrips around the country, barnstorming can be a lot better business now than it was back then."

"Makes you feel sort of powerful, doesn't it?" he said.

We walked out of Pecatonica for the last time, past a dog sitting chained to his doghouse. He had barked at us before. "How many times is the dog going to bark, Stu?"

"The dog is going to bark two times."

"I say the dog is going to bark four times. At least four times."

We walked by him and he didn't make a sound. He just sat there and watched our every move.

"Why, Stu, I believe the dog has come to know us!" I

stopped in the road and looked the dog in the eye. "He is now our friend!"

At that, the dog burst into barking, and by the time we were over the bridge, we had counted twelve full, rapid barks.

Stu found a half-size comic book lying by the road and picked it up. It was an advertising thing for Wrangler jeans, and it was all about Tex Marshall, rodeo star. Stu read aloud as we walked, acting out the parts of young Tex, starting his career as a bulldogger on the rodeo circuit. The theme of the story was Stay In School, Kids, documented by Tex's fierce will to get his college degree before turning full time to rodeo and earning a pile of money.

We wondered how that degree helped Tex hogtie Hereford calves in six seconds flat, but that was apparently something that all the guys take for granted. You get that degree, and you'll make more money in *any* job.

Again I urged Stu to get out of school until he decided what he wanted to do in the world, that he was just postponing living until he found that out, that it was doom to ever become a dentist if he was an adventurer at heart. He remained unconvinced.

We said goodbye to Skeeter, telling him that he was a good horse and we would remember him, and loaded the airplane. The engine warmed for the next adventure, beating back the tall grass in fifth-second impulses. It looked like a 1910 movie of a biplane running in tall grass, jerky and flickering.

By ten o'clock we were on a long run crosswind, dragging our shadow like a giant salmon fighting and thrashing at the end of a thousand-foot line. We didn't settle down to our next sight of Midwest America until the wheels touched and rolled on the grass of Kahoka, Missouri.

✄ CHAPTER FOURTEEN ✄

THERE WERE TWO BOYS and a dog, waiting.

"You in trouble, mister?"

"Nope, no trouble," I said.

"D'ja see me wavin' at you?"

"Didn't you see us wavin' back? You don't think we'd fly over and not wave, do you? Geemanee, what do you think we are, anyway?"

We unloaded our supply mountain and carried it across the deep green grass into the shade of a crumbling hangar. By the time we had the signs up and were open for business, there were eleven boys and seven bicycles scattered across the airplane and the grass.

It was an uncomfortable time. We didn't want to scare them all away, but neither did we want them walking through the fabric of the wings.

"Sure you can sit in the front seat, fellas, just stay on the black part of the wing, there, don't walk on the yellow. Careful, there." I turned to one boy looking soberly on. "How many people live in Kahoka, my friend?"

"Two thousand one hundred and sixty." He knew the exact figure.

There was a sharp explosion near the tail of the airplane and a little spray of grass jerked into the air. "Hey, fellas, let's keep the firecrackers away from the airplane, OK?"

There was some giggling and laughing from one knot of boys, and another explosion burst beneath the wingtip. More than anything at that moment, I felt like a junior-high teacher with a problem in discipline.

"NEXT GUY THROWS A FIRECRACKER BY THIS AIRPLANE I'M GONNA PICK UP AND THROW ACROSS THAT ROAD! YOU WANTA PLAY WITH THAT STUFF, YOU GET IT OUTA HERE!"

Violence worked at once. There were no more explosions in a hundred yards of the biplane.

Boys surged around us like pilot fish around sharks. When we walked clear of the airplane, everybody walked clear. When we leaned on the wing, everybody leaned on the wing. They were busy daring each other to fly . . . a giant challenge.

"I'd fly, if I had the money. I just don't have the money."

"If I loaned you three dollars, Jimmy, would you fly?"

"Nope," Jimmy said. "I wouldn't pay you back."

Their fear of the airplane was staggering. Every boy spoke of crashing; what do you do when the wings fall off . . . what if you jump and the chute doesn't open? There was going to be great disappointment in Kahoka if we didn't dive into the ground with at least one fatality.

"I thought you were all brave guys," Stu said. "And here nobody's got the courage to go up one time."

They gathered together, found that they could raise three dollars, and sent a spokesman. "If we paid you three dollars, mister, would you do some stunts for us?"

"You mean nobody goin' for a ride?" I said. "You all just watchin' from the ground?"

"Yeah. We'll pay you three dollars."

It was human society at work. If individual daring is ruled out, we can band together as spectators.

The boys all massed at the end of the strip, sitting down in the grass by the road. I taxied to the far end of the strip, so that we'd be taking off over their heads and toward town, all good advertising.

They were just little dots when the biplane's wheels lifted off the grass, but instead of climbing, we stayed low, skimming the grasstops, picking up speed and pointing straight into the young crowd.

If the engine quits here, I thought, we pull up, turn right and land in the bean field. But the boys didn't know this. All they could see was the biplane growing into a huge thing, roaring right straight at them, not turning, not climbing, coming bigger and louder than a five-ton firecracker.

They had just begun to scatter and dive for cover when we pulled steeply up and banked hard right, to keep the bean-field in gliding range.

We circled the town once for advertising, and then back over the strip we dropped down through loops and rolls and cloverleafs and a one-turn spin. The airshow lasted ten minutes, including the climb, and I waited to hear some general disappointment that three dollars could be shot up so fast.

"That was nice, mister!"

"Yeah! Gee, that part right at first, where you went zzzZZZZOOOOOOMM! right at us! That was scary!"

In a minute the first automobiles arrived, and we were glad to see them. Stu went into action, telling the joys of flying on a hot day like this, selling the idea of Kahoka from the cool, cool sky.

As Stu strapped him in, the first passenger said, "I want a thrill." A man walked to the cockpit just as we began to taxi out, and said in a low voice, "This fella is sort of the town cut-up. Take 'im up and turn 'im upside down a few times, OK?"

In every town we worked, all summer long, the one dominating personality was the watertower. In fact, the watertower became as much the symbol *Town* to us as it had become for the people who lived in its shadow. But now, up in the sun and the wind and the leather and the wires of the biplane, our passengers were for the first time looking down on that tower and its great black town-name painted.

I watched my riders carefully, at Kahoka, and every one of them looked long and thoughtfully at the top of the watertower, and then out to the road that led off over the horizon. It was part of the flight, when I saw this, to fly a separate little conquering circle over the shining four-pillared thing and its eight-foot letters KAHOKA. To rise above that tower was an event unforgotten.

By sundown we had flown nineteen passengers.

"What do I keep telling us, Stu," I said as we walked through the dark toward town. "We get right close in and we can't lose!"

We finished our hamburgers at the Orbit Inn and walked into the town square in the dark. The stores were closed, and silence drifted like slow fog in the branches of the elm trees.

There was a bandstand in the park, slope-roofed and faced about by rows of quiet wooden benches, all peaceful and silent in the warm summer night. The Seyb Emporium was across the way, and the sundries store, the hotel, with its wooden fans turning in the high lobby air. If I gave a dollar for every change in this square since 1919, I would still have been rich from the day's earnings.

We walked down the quiet sidewalks, back toward our field, listening to the faint strains of radio music rippling out from the yellow light of the houses.

The peace of Kahoka, however, did not extend to its mosquitoes. It was Erie all over again, and worse. At last I devised a Method D of Mosquito-Avoiding, which requires one to lie down fully clothed on a sleeping bag, throw a silken hammock over his head, and leave only a tiny hole for air. This worked fairly well, though it didn't spare me the hypersonic hum of a thousand tiny wings.

We were awake at the first cock-crow, about the time that the mosquitoes retired for the day.

I got up and poured a couple quarts of oil into the engine and looked it over well; we might have a busy day, close in. I had just closed the cowl when a car stopped by the field, sifting a cloud of fine flour-dust up from the dirt road.

"Are you flying yet, this morning?"

"Yes ma'am. All ready to start engines for you."

"I missed you yesterday and I was afraid you might leave . . ." She was a schoolteacher, there was no question about it. She had that kind of confidence and control over the world that comes only from forty years of channeling American history into ten thousand high-school pupils.

The 90-mile wind over the morning town destroyed the set of her silver-blue hair, but she gave no heed. She looked down on Kahoka and out toward the horizon farms exactly as children did, without any consciousness of herself at all.

Ten minutes later she gave Stu three one-dollar bills, thanked us both, and left in a slow trail of summer dust.

There is America, I thought. There is real frontier America, reflected in daughters a hundred years removed from her pioneers.

"What do you think of that?" Stu said. "I think we're in for a good day when they start coming out this early to fly."

"What's the estimate?" I began the walk toward town and breakfast. "How many passengers today?"

"I'll say . . . twenty-five. We'll fly twenty-five people today," Stu said, falling into step.

"Aren't we optimistic, this morning. Oh, it'll be a good day, for sure, but not that good. We'll fly eighteen people."

We were joined at the restaurant by one of our passengers of the day before, one Paul, by name, who owned a drag strip on the road out of town.

"Have a cup of coffee with you, for just a minute here," he said.

I was reflecting at the moment that there is nothing so horrible in the world as a stale glazed doughnut for breakfast.

"Always wanted to fly," Paul said. "Always wanted to, but never got around to it. At first, my folks were against me flyin', then my wife was thumbs down. But last night I kind of got the go-ahead to go again."

The doughnut was modifying my thinking. What would the world be like if we all had to have permission from wives and family before we did anything that we wanted to do; if we were all required to committee-think our desires? Would it be a different world, or are we living in one that is pretty much that way right now? I refused to believe that we were, and put the doughnut into the ash tray.

"You should get old Kenny up. Man, he would just go wild in that thing! I'm gonna bring him out. Bring 'im out tonight! I'm gonna see you guys get a good crowd . . . it's a fine thing, your comin' here. That little old airport just sits out there and nobody cares about it. Used to have a flying club with a couple airplanes, but they all lost interest and now there's just one plane left. You might get it goin' again."

Paul left in a few minutes, and we walked out into the sun-heat of July Missouri. A farm tractor drove swiftly by the square, its huge rear wheels singing on the pavement.

By ten-thirty business was going strong. One young man

flew four times, firing rolls of color film through his Polaroid camera. He was leaving to join the Army in two weeks, and he spent his money as though he had to get rid of it all before the two weeks was up. I was reminded of the gay and happy lives of the young Kamikaze pilots a few years back . . . this poor fellow was going to be heartbroken if he somehow managed to survive his first week in the Army.

Next to fly was a giant of a man, and he was clutching a plastic bag full of candy bars. "Hey, Dick," he said, reading my name on the cockpit rim. "How much you charge me to fly out over my farm, so I can toss these down to my kids? About nine miles north on State 81."

"Gee. That's 18 miles round-trip . . . 'd cost you . . . fifteen dollars. Awful steep price, but you see, whenever we go out of the local area . . ."

"Nothin' wrong with that price. That's fine. Kids'll go crazy, see their ol' dad comin' over in an airplane . . ."

In five minutes we had left Kahoka behind and were chugging over the softly rolling hills and gentle farmland south of the Des Moines River. He pointed the way, and at last down to a white farmhouse set a half-mile back from the road.

We dropped lower and circled the house, and the chugging roar of the Whirlwind brought his wife and children running out to see. He waved hard at them, and they all waved back, two-handedly. "GO RIGHT OVER 'EM!" he shouted, holding up the candy-bag so I'd get the idea.

The biplane settled 50 feet above the cornfield, and came streaking in over the little crowd on the ground. His arm moved, the candy-bag hurtled down. Children were on it like mongeese, lightning-fast, and sprang up to wave again to their dad. We circled twice and he signaled to return.

I had never flown with a more satisfied customer. He had the smile of Santa himself, aloft in a red and yellow sleigh in the middle of summertime. He had come and gone as he had promised, the good little children were all happy, and now the story could come to a close.

But there was plenty of work waiting for the sleigh when we returned.

An elderly skeptic finally agreed to fly, but reminded me, "None of them dadoes, now, 'member. Keep 'er nice and smooth."

It was a nice and smooth flight, until we were gliding down final approach to land. My passenger picked that time to suddenly begin waving his arms and shouting wildly.

I nodded and smiled, intent on landing, and didn't hear him until we had rolled to a stop once again by the road. "What was the matter?" I said. "Something go wrong up there? What were you tryin' to say?"

"HOO-*EE!*" he said, with the astonished smile of one who has cheated death. "Way we was comin' down, there, all turnin' and angled up . . . hoo-*ee!* I saw we was gonna land right in the pond, so I hollered, STRAIGHTEN 'ER OUT, BOY, *STRAIGHTEN 'ER OUT!* And you pulled 'er out just in time."

The day was full hot, and as long as the engine was running, there was a flock of boys standing in the cool hurricane behind the tail of the biplane. They were all young trout in the river of air, flopping around happily whenever I pushed the throttle forward to taxi out. Between passengers, I put my goggles up and relaxed, myself, in the breeze over the cockpit.

Once, when I landed, Stu was talking with a pair of news reporters. They were interested in the airplane and in us; they asked questions, took pictures. "Thanks a lot," they said as they left. "You'll be on the ten-twenty local news."

We flew passengers on and off all afternoon, but this was our second day at Kahoka, and it was time to think about moving on.

"I'm torn between staying here and making money," Stu said, "and moving on and making more."

"Then let's stay on tonight and push off tomorrow, early."

"Hate to leave a good spot. But we can always come back, can't we?"

We lay in the heated afternoon shade of the wing, trying to escape into the cool of sleep. There was a small sound in the sky.

"Airplane," Stu said. "Hey, look. Doesn't that look familiar?"

I looked. Way up overhead there was a yellow Cub circling, looking down. It turned, dropped swiftly down, pulled up in a loop and around in a roll. It was the same Cub that had flown with the five-plane Great American, at Prairie du Chien.

"That's Dick Willetts!" I said. "That's . . . now how did he know . . . sure, that's him!"

A few minutes later the Cub was down on the grass, rolling to a stop beside us. A good sight. Dick was a tall, calm and very skillful pilot, a reminder of how lonely it was to barnstorm with one single airplane.

"Hi! Thought I might find you down this way, somewhere."

"How'd you know where we were? You call Bette or something? How'd you find us?"

"I don't know. Just thought you might be around here," Dick said, sitting relaxed in the Cub's cockpit, puffing slowly on his pipe. "This was the last place I was going to try, really."

"Hm. That's fantastic."

"Yeah. How's it goin', barnstormin'?"

Dick stayed and flew through the afternoon with us, and

carried five passengers. I had a chance to stay on the ground and listen to the people after they had flown, and discovered that there is a great driving force toward believing that the pilot that one flies with is the best pilot in the world.

"Could you feel it when he landed?" one man said. "I couldn't feel when he landed. I could hear it, but I couldn't feel it, it was so smooth."

"Y'know, I have a lot of faith in him . . ."

"What do you think of your pilot, Ida Lee?" a coveralled farmer asked his wife, after she had flown with Dick.

"Everything was so pretty, and fun," she said. "I'd say he's *good*."

Just before five p.m. I saw that my fuel was getting too low to last through the heavy flying till sunset, and at the same time we found that the man who had the key to the gas pump was out of town.

"I'll hop over to Keokuk, Richard," I said, "and you keep the folks happy, flyin'."

"Take your time," he said.

In twenty minutes I was looking down in dismay at the Keokuk airport. It was all concrete runway, with new construction everywhere. To land on the hard surface would be to grind the tailskid to nothing, and I didn't have enough fuel to find another airport. But there was one short section of grass left on the west side of the field, and we landed there.

We had to cross a new runway to reach the pumps, all along the edge of the runway was a muddy deep ditch, with a five-inch lip of concrete to jump. We taxied back and forth along the edge of the runway, picked the least muddy section for crossing, and charged at it straight on.

It didn't work. The mud slowed the biplane to a walk, and by the time we reached the concrete lip, full power on the engine wasn't enough to drag it across.

I shut down the Wright, holding unkind thoughts about

aeronautical progress and the wholesale destruction of the grass runway, vowed never again to land at Keokuk or any modern airport, and went for a towing machine.

A tractor, mowing grass, was the answer.

"Hi!" I said to the driver. "Got a little problem here, trying to cross your new runway. Think that machine of yours could tow me out?"

"Oh, sure. She can tow airplanes ten times that size."

He left his grass-mowing at once and we rode together back to the airplane. When we got there, there was a line service man from the flight school across the field, looking in the cockpit.

"Looks like you got stuck," he said.

"Yes, sir," I said. "But we'll have 'er out in a minute here and I'll come over get some gas from you." I took a coil of stout rope from the tractor and tied it from the iron hitch to the landing gear of the biplane. "That oughta do 'er. We'll kinda help the wingtips here and you see if that tractor can do the job."

"Aw, she'll do the job. Don't you worry."

The tractor made it look easy. In a few seconds the biplane was standing free on the concrete, ready to start engine and taxi for gas.

"Thanks. You really saved me, sir."

"Think nothin' of it. She can pull airplanes ten times that big."

The line service man was looking nervously at the big steel propeller, hoping that I wouldn't ask him to swing that by hand to start the engine. It is a frightening thing to one who has never hand-propped a Wright, but we had no choice; the starting crank was in Kahoka.

"Why don't you hop in the cockpit, here," I said, "and I'll swing the prop." I walked back as he climbed aboard and showed him the throttle and ignition switch and brakes. "Just pull the throttle back a bit after she starts," I said. "She should start right off."

I pulled the propeller through a few times, and said, "OK, give me contact and brakes, and we'll start her goin'."

I pulled the big blade down and the engine fired at once. Good old reliable Wright.

I was walking casually toward the cockpit when I saw that the man in the pilot's seat was frozen in horror, and that the engine was much louder than it should have been. The throttle was nearly full open, and in all the wind and sudden noise, my helper had forgotten what to do. He sat there, staring straight ahead, as the biplane, all by herself, began to move.

"THE THROTTLE!" I screamed. "CUT THE THROTTLE!" Quick visions flashed of the Parks leaping into the air with a man at the controls who had no faintest idea how to fly. I ran toward the cockpit, but already the airplane was rolling swiftly across the concrete, engine roaring wildly. It was a dream, like running from a railroad train. I threw myself desperately at the cockpit, grabbed the leather rim with one hand, but could not move any farther. The immense propellerblast kept me from moving; it was all I could do to race alongside the biplane.

The vision of my airplane a total wreck gave me one burst of strength to claw my way against the hurricane, up onto the wing. We were moving 20 miles an hour, accelerating quickly. I clung to the edge of the cockpit with every ounce of strength I could squeeze from my body. The man was cold wax in the seat, his eyes glazed, his mouth open.

The biplane was moving far too fast, and turning, now. We were going to groundloop. In one desperate motion I reached over the cockpit rim, grabbed the throttle and slammed it back. It was too late, and all I could do was hold on as we went around. The tires cried out, dragging sideways, one wing lifted, the other went hard down, scraping concrete. I clung there and waited for a wheel to collapse, or the gear to break away.

After five seconds tense as shredding steel, the wings leveled and we coasted to a stop, all in one piece.

"That," I said, panting, "was a ground loop."

The man climbed like a robot from the cockpit, and not one word did he say. He set his feet on the ground and began walking woodenly toward the office. It was the last I saw of him.

The engine was still running. I set myself down into the seat and talked to the biplane for a while. This had been her way of telling me not to leave her to unknowing people, and I promised that I would never let that happen again.

It was nearing sundown by the time we landed at Kahoka, and Dick was ready to leave.

"I gotta get goin'," he said. "I told my wife I'd be home at seven, and it's seven right now. I shall do some violent aerobatics over the field and be on my way. Let me know when you're back around here."

"Thanks, Richard. We'll do 'er."

I propped the Cub for him and he was off. He flew a pretty set of aerobatics overhead, as he promised, plus a few strange things of his own—flying sideways through the air, flat turns, steep climbs and pushovers.

The crowd was on us before Dick had disappeared in the west, and we flew the last hour steadily, till dark. By the time we covered the airplane and walked to the Orbit Inn, we felt as if we had been working for a living. We had flown twenty-six passengers by the end of the day, and Dick had flown another five. He had made his gas-and-oil money, and Stu and I split $98.

"Almost made it, Stu. Almost broke a hundred-dollar day." We felt affluent, and ordered double milkshakes.

Stu was worried that we would miss the ten-twenty local news, so we walked into the hotel lobby and found the antique television set going unwatched.

It was an interesting lobby. The fans washed mild vertical air down over us, in reminder of times that hadn't quite gone by. There was a bell on the counter, the kind that dings when you tap the button on the top. Against the wall was a monster Firestone Air Chief radio console, four feet high and three feet wide, with stick-on paper squares over the pushbuttons: WGN, WTAD, WCAZ. If I pressed those buttons, I wondered, would I find Fred Allen, strolling in gentle static down Allen's Alley; or Jack Armstrong, the All-American Boy; or Edgar Bergen and Charlie McCarthy? I was afraid to try.

The ten-twenty news came and went without any mention of those delightful barnstormers out by the edge of Kahoka, and Stu was crushed. "My one chance to get on television! One chance! And I ended up on the newsroom floor!"

That night Stu tried using cheesecloth for a mosquito net, taping a peak of it to the bottom of the wing. From what I could see in the dark it looked good, but it didn't work. The mosquitoes learned at once that the trick was to land, to walk under the edge of the net, then take to the air once they were inside. It was another hard night.

As we settled sleepily into the breakfast booth, I said, "Well, Stu, is it moving-on time?"

"Oi thonk so," he said, yawning. " 'Scuse me. Darn mosquitoes."

We were blessed with a charming waitress, who had somehow missed her Warner Brothers screen test. "What are we having for breakfast this morning?" she asked sweetly.

"Cherry pancakes, please," I said, "bunch of 'em, with honey."

She wrote the order, and stopped. "We don't have cherry pancakes. Is that on the menu?"

"No. Awful good, though."

She smiled. "We'll give you cherry pancakes if you get the cherries," she said.

I was out the door in a flash, into the market two doors down, and laying out 29 cents for a can of cherries. The waitress was still at the table when I returned, and I set the can down triumphantly. "You just take these and dump 'em right in the batter."

"The whole can?"

"Yes, ma'm. Zonk. Right in the batter. Great pancakes."

"Well . . . I'll ask the cook . . ."

A moment after she left, I noticed that we had company. "Stu, there is an ant on our table."

"Ask him where we're going to go today." He unfolded the road map.

"Here you go, little fella," I said, and helped the ant onto the map. "This is known as the Ant Method of Navigation, Mister MacPherson. You just follow after him with a pen, now. Wherever he goes, we go."

The ant was frightened, and traveled east across Missouri at a great rate. He stopped, wandered nervously south, turned west, stopped, turned northeast. The line under Stu's pen passed some promising towns, as he followed, but then the ant struck out due east, toward the sugar bowl. He stepped across a fold in the map, and in that one step covered 300 miles, all the way across southern Illinois. Then he leaped off the map and ran for the sugar.

We consumed our magnificent cherry pancakes and looked at the line. Up to the fold, the ant had a pretty good plan. Push east and south, swing around in a big circle to end at Hannibal, Missouri. We'd get a taste of southern Illinois, and the county fair season was upon us as summer burned on. There might be some good places to work, at the fairs.

Decision made, water jug filled, we said goodbye to our waitress, tipping her for being pretty, and walked to the plane.

In half an hour we were off again, pushing into a headwind. The ant had not told us about headwinds. The longer we flew, the more annoyed I got at that dumb ant. There was nothing down there. A few little towns with no place to land, an isolated Army outpost, a million acres of farmland. If there was sugar to the east, we certainly weren't finding it.

There was a fair in progress at Griggsville, Illinois, but no place to land, except in a wheatfield adjacent. The gold of that wheat was no illusion. At the going wheat prices, it would cost us $75 to roll down a landing-swath of the tall grain.

We flew on, and days passed, and our affluence dwindled.

There was a fair at Rushville, with horses and sulkies trotting stiffly around the quarter-mile, and crowds of potential passengers. But there was no place to land. We circled dismally overhead, and finally pushed on, cursing the ant.

At last we staggered into Hannibal, and talked with Vic Kirby, an old barnstormer who ran the airport there. We stayed a while with him, bought some gas at discount because all antique planes get discounts at Hannibal, and then at his suggestion, flew north to Palmyra, Missouri.

There was no comparison to Palmyra, Wisconsin, which was centuries away now, in the distant past. This strip was short and narrow, lined by farm equipment and tall corn. We stopped long enough to fly one passenger, and then were off again, aimlessly south, weaving back and forth across the Mississippi, then east again into Illinois.

Landing in a grass field at Hull, I figured we had set a record for biplane crossings of the Mississippi in one day.

We sold three quick rides in the town of five hundred souls, and found that the hayfield we had landed upon had only the day before been approved by the State of Illinois as a landing area. The flying club was going strong, volunteer-building a cement-block office.

"You're the first airplane to land here since this field became an airport!" We heard it over and over again, and we were told it was an honor. But it was ironic. We wanted to have nothing to do with airports, we were just looking for little grassy places to land on, and here our hayfield had been declared an airport beneath our very wheels.

Flying all that day long, using two full tanks of gas, we had earned a total of twelve dollars cash.

"I don't know, Stu. 'Cept for Pecatonica, Illinois just don't seem to be our piece of cake, huh? Next thing you know, ol' what's-his-name is gonna be down here askin' about our Illinois registration tag."

Stu mumbled something, rigged his useless mosquito net and flopped down on his sleeping bag. "You were born in this state, weren't you?" he said, and was asleep at once. I never did figure out what that remark was supposed to mean.

♛ CHAPTER FIFTEEN ♛

I WOKE UP at six-thirty in the morning, to the click of a Polaroid camera-shutter. A man was taking pictures of us sleeping under the wing.

"Mornin'," I said. "Feel like flyin' this mornin'?" It was more reflex than a hunger for three dollars.

"Maybe in a little while. Takin' some pictures now. You don't mind, do you?"

"No." I dropped my head down on my hammock-pillow and went back to sleep.

We woke up again at nine, and there was a crowd standing a discreet distance away, looking at the airplane.

One fellow looked at me strangely, and studied the name painted by the cockpit rim.

"Say," he said at last. "You wouldn't be the Dick Bach that writes for the flying magazines, would you?"

I sighed. Goodbye, Hull, Illinois. "Yeah. I do a little story, once in a while."

"How do you like that. Why don't you stand over by the cockpit, there, and I'll get your picture."

I stood, glad that he liked my stories, but no longer the anonymous barnstormer.

"Let's pack up, Stu."

Illinois in midsummer was a scenic green hazy oven, and we droned through the broiled air like a worried bee. We wandered north on the Illinois River for days, finding no profit. And then one afternoon a city flowed in from the horizon. Monmouth, Illinois. Population 10,000. Airport north.

Stu looked back at me as we circled the city and I shrugged. It was a sod field, anyway, we could say that much for it. The question was whether a city this size would be interested in barnstormers.

We'd find out, I thought. We'd work it just as if it was a little town. We landed, taxied to the gas pump and stopped the engine.

There was a row of nine airplanes parked, and a large brick hangar with an antique steam locomotive inside.

The man who drove out to unlock the pump was an old-timer who had worked at Monmouth Airport for thirty years. "I seen it when there was six, eight instructors here," he said. "Thirty people here at one time, a whole big line of airplanes. Had another runway, then, too, out into where that cornfield is now. This is the oldest continuous-used airport in Illinois, you know. Since 1921."

By the time he unloaded us at the restaurant, a half-mile from the airport, we had learned something about the way things were in Monmouth aviation. A glory that was past; once the stopping-place for the glittering names of flight, now the quiet resort of a few weekend pilots.

In the frosted air of the restaurant, the name "Beth" began our list of Monmouth Knowns. She was interested in the airplane, but she brought us little hope with our hamburgers.

"Summer's the wrong time for you. All the kids from the

college are gone home." There was a long silence, and she smiled sadly for us and left us alone.

"So," said Stu, tired. "No kiddies. Where do we go from here?"

I named some places, none of which were much more promising than Monmouth. ". . . and as a very last resort, we could try Muscatine."

"Sounds too much like Mosquito." That spiked Muscatine.

"Well, heck. Let's just work Monmouth and see what happens. Give it a chance, you know. Might do a jump, maybe, see if we can get the people out."

The jump was first priority. By the time we had the airplane unpacked and ready to work, it was five o'clock, the best time for crowd-attracting.

Stu jumped from 3500 feet, down into horizonless haze, moving at meteor-speed toward the runway grass. His canopy snapped open in a great poof of white, the last of the King's Ransom packed into the folded nylon, and now he drifted downward like a small tired cumulus cloud.

While we dived to circle him, I saw a few cars gathering, but not nearly so many as I expected from a town that size. We flew some mild aerobatics over the cornfields and landed. Stu had logged another good jump, and I taxied to find him working the cars, saying over and again how cool was the air at 3500 feet.

The people didn't want to fly. "That thing state-inspected?" I heard one man ask, looking at the biplane.

We're a long way from small-town flying, I thought. It sounds as if city people live in the present day, as if they live at modern speeds and expect modern guarantees for their safety. We carried two passengers by sundown.

The local pilots were very kind, and promised bigger crowds the next day. "We had a parachute meet here a month ago, and there were cars backed all the way up to the main highway," they said. "Just takes a little while for the word to get around."

By the time we walked into the restaurant for supper, I was having doubts all over again about Monmouth.

"Stu, what do you think about pressing on, tomorrow? This place feel right to you?"

"Two rides. That's normal first-day, you know."

"Yeah, but the place just doesn't seem with it, you know? In the little towns, we're a big thing, and people at least come out to look. Here we're just another airplane. Nobody cares." We ordered from Beth, who gave us a happy smile and said that she was glad to see us back.

"Might as well give the place a try," Stu said. "We hunted a long time, remember. Some other places looked bad, too, at first."

"OK. We'll stay." Another day, at least, would confirm my fears about big-city barnstorming. It just did not feel comfortable; we were out of our element, out of our time.

Stu and I slept in the airport office that night. There were no mosquitoes.

It plagued me all through the next day. We carried passengers well, until by seven o'clock we had flown eighteen rides, but the spirit of barnstorming was gone. We were just a couple of crazy guys selling airplane rides.

At seven, a man came to us as we sat under the wing.

"Hey, fellas, I wonder if you could do something a little special for me."

"Speak special speak," I said in archaic Air Force slang. Stu and I had been talking about Air Force life.

"I'm having a party over at my house . . . wonder if I could hire you to give us a little airshow. We're just on the edge of town, right over there."

"Doubt if you'd see much," I said. "My minimum altitude

is fifteen hundred feet above the ground, and I'd start at three thousand. Be just a little speck to you, is all."

"That doesn't make any difference. Could you give us a show for say . . . twenty-five dollars?"

"Sure thing, if you want it. But I'm not coming down less than fifteen hundred feet."

"Fine." He took two tens and a five-dollar bill from his wallet. "Could you be up at seven-thirty?"

"No problem. You keep your money, though. If you think it was worth it, you can stop by and give us the money tomorrow. If you don't like it, don't bother."

At seven-thirty we were over the cornfields at the edge of town, and starting our first loop. By seven-forty the show was over, and we circled down over the park to watch the baseball game.

When we landed, Stu had two passengers ready to go.

"Give us a wild ride!" they said.

They got the Standard Wild Ride; steep turns, sideslips, with the wind smashing over them, dives and zooms. They were as gay and excited in the air as though the biplane was the biggest fastest roller-coaster in the world, and all of a sudden I was surprised at it. During the minutes we had been flying, I was thinking about moving out of Monmouth, and wondered where we might go next. I wasn't seeing the ride as wild or the Parks as a roller-coaster. Fun, perhaps, in a mild sort of way, and interesting, but hardly exciting.

A revelation, that, and a warning of evil. The summer was beginning to go stale, I was taking even the strange and adventurous life of a gypsy pilot for granted, and as just another job.

I pulled the airplane up into a half-roll, which set them to clutching the leather cockpit-rim in fearful delight, and talked out loud to myself. "Hey listen, Richard! That's the wind! Hear it through the wires, feel it on your face, beating these goggles! Wake up! This is here and now, and time for you to be alive! Snap out of it! See! Taste! Wake up!"

All at once I could hear again . . . the blast and concussion of the Whirlwind went from an unheard Niagara to the roar of a wild old engine again, a highspeed metronome firing dynamite with each beat of its blade.

That magnificent perfect sound . . . how long had it been since I had ceased to listen to it? Weeks. That sun, bright as incandescent steel in a blue-fire sky . . . how long since I had leaned back my head and held the taste of that sun in my mouth? I opened my eyes and looked right up into it and drank the heat of it. I took off one glove and grabbed a handful of wind, never breathed by anybody in ten billion years, and I grabbed it and snuffed it deep within me.

The people ahead of you, Richard, open your eyes! Who are they? Look at them! See! They changed at once from passengers into living people, a young man, a young woman, bright and happy and beautiful in the way that we are all beautiful when we are for a moment completely unconscious of ourselves, when we are looking out toward something that absorbs us completely.

We banked again, steeply, and they looked together down fifteen feet of brilliant lemon wings and nine hundred feet of hard transparent air and five feet of corn-plant sea and a tenth-inch of black loam, stuffed with minerals. Wings, air, corn, loam, minerals and birds and lakes and roads and fences and cows and trees and grass and flowers—every bit of it moved in a great sweeping stroke of colors, and the colors went in through the wide open eyes of these fellow-people of mine, and deep into their hearts, to surface in a smile or a laugh and the brave beautiful look of those who have not yet chosen to die.

Never stop being a kid, Richard. Never stop tasting and feeling and seeing and being excited with great things like

air and engines and the sounds of sunlight within you. Wear
your little mask, if you must, to protect the kid from the
world, but if you let that kid disappear, buddy, you are grown
up and you are dead.

The tall old wheels rumbled and thumped on earth soft
as a giant petrified pillow, and the flight, the first ride for my
passengers and the thousandth for me, was over. They became
conscious of themselves again and said thank you that was
great and paid Stu six dollars and got into their automobile
and drove away. I said thank you, it's been nice flying with
you, and I was absolutely dead certain that we would all remember our flight together for a very long time.

That night, Stu and I laid out the couch cushions into
islands of soft on the office floor, cast mild and pleasant wrath
upon the man who never returned to pay us for our $25 air-
show, and settled down with strawberry soda pop in mos-
quitoless air. The only light in the room came from the sun,
reflected off the moon bright enough to show the colors of
the biplane outside.

"Stuart Sandy MacPherson," I said. "Who the devil are
you?"

The boy's mask of solemn quiet was more and more clearly
a pure fake, for quiet solemn people do not jump from the
wings of airplanes a mile in the air, or travel half-way across
the country to become a barnstormer. Even Stu realized that
the question was in order, and didn't dodge it.

"Sometimes I'm not too sure who I am," he said. "I was
on the varsity tennis team, in high school, if that helps you
very much. I did some mountain climbing . . ."

I blinked. "You mean regular mountain climbing? With
the ropes and pitons and crampons and rock walls and all
that? Or do you mean just hills that you can walk up?"

"The whole works. It was fun. Until I got hit on the head

with a rock. Knocked me out for a while. I was lucky I was roped to the guy ahead of me."

"You were just dangling there in space, at the end of a rope?"

"Yeah."

"Boy."

"Yeah. Well, then I quit mountain climbing and took up flying. Got my private license. Flying Piper Cubs."

"Stu! Why didn't you say you had your license? You know, my gosh! You're supposed to tell us things like that!"

I thought, in the darkness, that he shrugged.

"I did a lot of motorcycle-riding. It's fun, to try to be good with a machine . . ."

"Fantastic, kid!" The nice thing about not talking very much is that when you do talk, you can startle people so much that they listen. "Now. Look," I said. "I've heard of some pretty dumb things, some people who really sold themselves down the river, but you take the cake, about. You have all these great things going for you, like a real live person, and yet there you are in Salt Lake at Dentist School. Please tell me . . . *why?*"

He set his pop bottle down with a heavy clink on the floor. "I owe it to my folks," he said. "They've paid my way . . ."

"You owe it to your folks to be happy. Don't you? They've got no right to force you into something where you aren't happy."

"Maybe." He thought for a moment. "Maybe that's the trouble . . . it's too easy to stay in the system, the way things are. If I did drop out, I'd get sucked up in the draft, and then where would I be?"

"Ah—Stu?" I said. I wanted to talk about his school, but the last words frightened me. "What's patriotism, do you imagine? What do you think it means?"

There was the longest silence then, that I had heard all

summer. The boy was trying, he was turning it over and over in his mind. And he was coming up with nothing. I lay there and listened to him think, wondering if the same emptiness was in the minds of all the other college youth around the country. If it was, the United States of America was facing some more difficult times.

"I don't know," he said at last. "I don't know . . . what . . . patriotism . . . is."

"No wonder you're scared of the draft, then, fella," I snapped. "This patriotism stuff is three words: Gratitude. For. Country. You go out, climb your mountains, you drive your motorcycles; I can fly wherever I want, write what I want to write, and I can jump all over the government whenever it's being stupid. How many guys do you think have been shot all to bits so you and I can run our lives the way we want? Hundred thousand guys? Million guys?"

Stu sat on the pillows, his hands clasped behind his head, looking across the dark room.

"So we take a year or two or five out of this fantastic freedom," I said, "and we say, 'Hey, country, thanks!' "

At that moment I wasn't talking to Stu MacPherson, but to all my poor vacant young countrymen who couldn't understand, whining about the draft in the midst of sacred rare beautiful liberty.

I wanted to box them all up and ship them to some slave nation, and make them stay there until they were ready to fight their way back home. But if I nailed the crates down on them, I'd be destroying the very freedom I wished them to see. I had to let them whine, and pray they'd see the picture before they broke the country into jelly-blobs of self-pity.

Stu was silent. I didn't want him to talk. I prayed, very deeply, that in the silence, he was listening.

☙ CHAPTER SIXTEEN ☙

BY TEN O'CLOCK IN THE MORNING the oven Illinois was a kiln. The grass scorched beneath our feet. There was a very light hot breeze, a low oriental woodwind through the flying wires as we sat in the shade under the wing.

"OK, Stu-babe, here is a map. I shall take my knife and hurl it into the map. Wherever the knife hits, we go."

I tossed the knife down end over end, and to my surprise, the blade struck hard and firm through the map. A good omen. We checked the slit eagerly.

"Great," I said. "We are supposed to go land in the Mississippi River. Thanks a lot, knife."

We tried again and again, and the only result was a map full of holes. There was a reason not to fly to any place the knife suggested.

A car stopped, and a man and two boys walked toward us.

"When they get out of the car, they are already sold," Stu said. "Do we want to fly anybody today, or just get going?"

"Might as well fly 'em."

Stu went to work. "Hi, folks."

"You with the airplane?"

"Yes, sir!"

"We want to fly."

"Glad to have you aboard. Why don't you just step right over here . . ." He broke off in mid-sentence. "Hey, look, Dick. A biplane."

It came small and quiet, whispering in from the west, easing down toward us through the sky.

"Stu, that's a Travelair! That's Spencer Nelson! He made it!"

It was a bomb set off in our midst. I leaped into the cockpit and tossed the starting crank to Stu.

"You don't mind waiting a minute, folks, do you?" I said to the man and his sons. "This other airplane is all the way from California. I'll go up and welcome him in, and then we'll fly."

They didn't have a chance to protest. The engine, screaming from the inertia starter, burst into life and we were taxiing at once, gathering speed, lifting off the ground, turning toward the newcomer. He was swinging into the landing pattern when we caught him, and closed into formation alongside.

The pilot waved.

"HEY, SPENCE!" I shouted, knowing he couldn't hear a word over the wind.

His airplane was beautiful. It was just out of the shop, finished by this airline captain who couldn't get enough of flying. The machine shined and sparkled and flashed in the sunlight. There wasn't a single patch, not one oil-streak or spot of grease down its whole length, and I blinked at its perfection. The big air-balanced rudder touched over and we turned for a low pass along the grass runway.

Travelair Aircraft Co., went the smooth professional letters on the tail, *Wichita, Kansas*. The airplane was a sleek eager dolphin in the sky, a much larger machine than the Parks, and much more elegant. We felt like a seamy tar-

stained little tugboat nosing the *United States* into harbor.
I wondered if Spence knew what he was getting into, if his
glossy blue airplane was going to look as pretty going home
as it looked this minute.

We whistled once more through the pattern and landed,
that queen of a biplane leading the way, taxiing to the passengers, shutting down into a stately silence.

I had never met the pilot, and knew him only through
letters and telephone calls as he had struggled to get his airplane ready for the summer. When he took off his helmet
and climbed down from the high cockpit, I saw that Spencer
Nelson was a short quick man with the hawkish look of an
old-time pilot: firm angled face, intense blue eyes.

"Mister Nelson!" I said.

"Mister Bach, I presume?"

"Spence, you nutty guy. You made it! Where you in from
this morning?"

"In from Kearny, Nebraska. Five hours' flying. I called your
house, Bette said you had called from here." He stretched,
glad to be out of the cockpit. "That old parachute gets kind
of hard to sit on after a while, don't it?"

"Well, from here on out, you are in the land of happy
barnstorming, Spence. But you come out here to stand 'round
and talk, or you wanta do some work? We got passengers
waitin'."

"Let's go," he said.

He piled a mass of equipment from the front cockpit onto
the ground, and Stu led two of the passengers to the big airplane. I helped the other one into the Parks, which was looking rattier every moment she stood alongside the Travelair.

"I'll follow you," Spence called, as Stu cranked his engine
into blue smoke and roar.

We took off and fell into the Monmouth Barnstorming
Pattern, one long turn around the city, a circle over a little

lake west with sunsparkles on the water, and gliding turns to landing . . . ten minutes exactly. The Travelair was much faster than the Parks, and zoomed by her in the first turn after takeoff. Spence took far too long, making double turns and side excursions all over the place.

He landed five minutes after the Parks.

"Hey, what are you tryin' to do?" I said. "The people are not paying to ride along while you break the biplane endurance record, you know. They're paying to get a taste of the wind in the wires, and to see how it all looks from the air. I'd hate to have you for competition."

"Was that too long? I'll watch that. Just breakin' in here, you know."

We walked to the restaurant and heard his story of trials and frustration with officials and paperwork while he had put the finishing touches on the Travelair and raced across the country to catch us.

"I've only got five days left on my vacation, with all that delay at first. I'll have to be gettin' on home here in a couple days."

"Spence! You come all the heck way out here for *two days'* barnstorming? That is bad news! You are some kind of a nut, I hope to tell ya!"

He shrugged his shoulders. "Never been barnstorming before."

"Well, we sure got to get out of here, give you something a little more typical, and make you some money to get home on, anyway."

"How about Kahoka?" Stu said. "Remember they said they had drag races or some big thing coming up. Lots of people. Close to town."

"That's an airstrip, though. We want a good hayfield."

We thought it over for a while, and at last Stu prevailed.

With just two days left for our new pilot, we couldn't afford to wander aimlessly.

By three o'clock we were airborne, heading south and east into Missouri. Stu rode the Travelair front seat, and I had a cockpit full of baggage and parachutes.

We had a problem at once. The Travelair was too fast; Spence had to keep his power way back to fly slow enough for me to stay with him. Every once in a while he would forget, and think about something else, and then turn around to find a tiny speck of a Parks trailing a mile behind. But by the time we crossed the Mississippi, we were working together and our shadows flicked over the brown water in good formation. It was a fine feeling, not to be alone, to have another biplane out there going the same way through the old sky. We felt happy, my airplane and I, and we did a little swooping and turning just for fun.

A barnstormer, I found, gets to know the country well. It wasn't necessary to look once at the map. Head toward the sun till you hit the Mississippi. Fly down the river till you can see the Des Moines River coming in from the west. Cut north of Keokuk and angle a little south for ten minutes and there's Kahoka.

The drag strip was overflowing with people. We flew one circle to let the world know that we had arrived, and turned to land.

"Hey, this looks nice," Spence said as soon as we had landed. "Nice grass, town's right here, this looks real nice."

The passengers came at once and it was luxury to let the Travelair carry the first ones, just to sit on the ground and let Spence bring in the money.

We were big time now, with a Ship Number One and a Ship Number Two to work for us. Unfortunately I couldn't enjoy the luxury long, for greasy old Ship Number One had customers walking toward her, ready to fly. I climbed into my familiar seat and we were on our way through the afternoon. There were just a few hours left till sundown, but we worked straight through, and carried twenty-three riders before the day was over.

I heard bits and pieces of passenger-talk, between takeoffs.

"I been twenty-five years trying to get my wife off the ground, and today she finally goes up in that blue plane."

"This is real flying. The modern stuff is transportation, but this is real flying."

"Sure glad you guys showed up—it'll do a lot for this town."

It was like coming home, Kahoka. The Orbit Inn was still there and going strong, with its juke-box music; and the young people sitting on the fenders of their cars in the warm night air.

"This is fun," Spence said. "Not just the money, but talking to the people. You're really doing something for 'em."

Stu and I saw it all again for the first time, through the other pilot's eyes as he talked. It was good to see Spencer Nelson there in night Kahoka, carried away with the fresh new joys of barnstorming.

☙ CHAPTER SEVENTEEN ❧

"I GOT AN OIL LEAK!" Spence was concerned, and pointed to a tiny line of clean oil from the engine cowl.

"You want to trade oil leaks, Mister Nelson?" I said. "Now I've got a few nice leaks that you might find interesting . . ."

"Your engine's supposed to leak," he said. "But a Continental's supposed to be tight as a drum." He was worried, and loosened the Travelair's bottom cowl in the first rays of cool morning sunlight.

Oh, well, I thought, if we have early passengers, I'll do the flying. I dragged out my tool kit and we began checking over his big engine.

"Everything's so new," he said. "Probably just some fittings working in, and they're loose now."

Which was part of the trouble. Some of the oil-hose connections were loose enough to turn a full time around before snugging tight again.

"That ought to do her up," he said after half an hour's work. "Let's give her a try."

"I'll crank it for you." I set the starter crank into the side of the cowl and thought that it was a pretty light little fitting for the heavy crank.

"It's a bit flimsy there, that crank thing," Nelson said, from the cockpit. "When I get back I'm gonna beef that up."

I turned the crank three turns, and the shaft snapped off under my hand.

"What's the matter?" he called.

"Spence, kiddo, I think you're gonna have to beef this thing up before you get back."

"It didn't break, did it?"

"Yessir."

"Well, I'll find a place in town and get it all welded up. Just as soon get it out of the way now, huh?"

He took the shaft loose and set off for town. If this was to be his only maintenance problem in two days, he would be doing well indeed as a gypsy pilot.

A man drove up and looked at the airplanes. "You fly those?"

"Sure do," I said, walking over to the window of the Chevrolet. "You lookin' to ride today?"

"I don't know," he said, thoughtfully. Sitting next to him in the car was a completely beautiful young woman, with long black hair and very wide dark eyes.

"Town's awful pretty in the morning . . . air's nice and still and smooth," I said. "Cooler up there, too."

The man was interested, teetering on the brink of adventure, but the girl looked at me as a frightened doe would, and didn't make a sound.

"Think I should go up?" the man asked her.

There was no reply, not a single word. She shook her head the tiniest bit no.

"Never had a passenger who didn't think the ride was great—your money back if you don't like it." I surprised myself with that. I really didn't care if the man flew or not; there would be plenty of passengers later on. The money-back guarantee was a good stunt, but I hadn't even considered it until that second. It was a clash of my world against the world of that girl, and the man was our battleground.

"I think I'll go. Take long?"

"Ten minutes." I had won, that quickly.

"Be right back," he said to the girl. She looked at him with her deep dark eyes, afraid, but still she didn't say a word.

We flew ten minutes, and because I was curious, I kept looking back and down, as we flew, at the Chevrolet. The car door did not open, there was no face looking up through the window. Something strange about that woman, and the bright summer day went eerie and uncomfortable.

The landing was normal, every bit normal, like every landing we made those days. We were down and rolling along the grass, moving perhaps 40 miles per hour. Suddenly a voice spoke within me: "Move it over to the right, swing out to the right." There was no reason to do it, but I did, wondering that I would.

In that instant, as the biplane moved right, an airplane flashed past on our left, landing in the opposite direction on the grass, moving perhaps 50 miles per hour.

For a second I was stunned, a sheet of cold went through me. I hadn't seen the other plane, he clearly hadn't seen me. If we hadn't moved to the right, the biplane's barnstorming days would have come to a very quick, spectacular end. The other plane turned, lifted again into the air, and disappeared. I thanked that voice, that angel-thought, and since the incident was all over I would best be very casual about it, or better, not speak of it at all.

The man handed Stu three dollar bills and got back into his car. The girl had not moved, she had not spoken.

"Thanks a lot," my passenger said, happy, and with his strange strange person, drove away. We didn't see them again.

•   •   •

Spence came back with a welded starter shaft of solid iron, strong enough to hang his whole airplane from.

"This ought to do the job," he said. "Let's try her again."

The engine fired at once and he was off for a test flight. When he returned ten minutes later, there was still a faint spray of oil from the crankcase breather.

"Well, gee," he said. "I'd sure like to get rid of that oil."

"Spence, that's the *breather!* That is oil *mist,* you're talking about. I don't know too many barnstormers who worry about oil mist on their airplanes. All we care about here is that the wings are on good and tight, you know?"

"OK. But still, I don't like it on my pretty new Travelair."

Spence got the next two passengers, a man and his boy. When they were strapped aboard, he lowered his goggles, pushed the throttle forward and started his takeoff across the grass. I turned to Stu. "Sure is nice to have somebody else to do the work, so we . . ." I stopped in mid-sentence, stricken. The Travelair engine had quit on takeoff.

"Oh, no." This, I thought, in a tenth of a second, is not our day.

The big airplane glided down again to the grass, rolling soundlessly toward the far end of the strip; the engine had stopped soon enough to allow a quick safe landing.

In a second it cut in again, purring smoothly, but Spence didn't try another takeoff. He taxied straight back toward us.

"Wonder what the passengers think of that," Stu said, with a faint smile.

I opened the cockpit door for them when the biplane arrived. "Kind of a short ride, wasn't it?" I said, sounding cool. It would have terrified me, if I were in the front seat when everything stopped.

"Oh, it was long enough, but we didn't get very high," the man said, helping his son down to the grass. It was a remarkable thing to say, and I was proud of him.

"You want to ride in Ship Number One?"

"No, thanks. We'll give you a chance to fix this one . . . be back tonight and fly."

I accepted this as a brave excuse, and crossed them off the list of passengers who would ever trust a biplane. When they had left, we got to work.

"Clearly, the thing isn't getting any gas, to stop like that," I said.

"Dirt in the gas?" Spence said.

"Sounds good. Let's give it a try."

The engine had been stored in Arizona, and there was a teaspoonful of sand in the fuel strainer.

"That's part of the problem, anyway," Spence said. "Let's try it again."

We tried again, but the engine would sputter and cough at full throttle, then cut out completely.

"How's your fuel?"

"Oh, I got half a tank." He thought of something and ran the engine up again. It worked perfectly. "Centersection tank," he said. "It works fine if it's running on gas out of the high tank."

He experimented with it and found that there was nothing he could do to make the engine quit as long as it was taking fuel out of the big overhead tank buried in the middle of the top wing.

"That's it," he said at last. "Float level or something in the carburetor isn't quite right. She wants that extra pressure when she's going full throttle."

The problem was solved and we celebrated with a parachute jump. Stu was anxious to enter a "Travelair Jump" in his sky-diver's logbook, and we were airborne in midafternoon, flying formation on the way up to jump altitude.

I broke away at 2,500 feet and circled to wait for Stu to come down.

We could expect heavy business if the parachute jump went as planned; the dragstrip crowd was out in force. But it didn't go quite as planned. Stu missed his target. I followed him down, knowing that from my angle I couldn't tell where he was going to land. But the lower he got, the clearer it was that he wouldn't make the runway, and that he might end up in the telephone wires across the weedlot to the south.

He missed the wires by a few feet and was down in the weeds, then up again, waving that he was OK. Spence and I flew a formation advertising flight, broke apart and landed. There was a crowd waiting to fly, and Stu was just panting onto the field, carrying his parachute.

"Man! I thought I got those wires! I waited around too long before I did anything about the wind. Bad jump!" But that was it. We avoid disaster and we go on working.

He dumped the chute on his sleeping bag and was selling rides at once. I nodded here-we-go to Spence and we got into the airplanes. Again we didn't stop flying till sundown. To my great surprise, Spence's engine-failure passengers, the man and his boy, came back to fly again. This time the Continental kept on running for them, and they saw Kahoka from the air, a town sailing serenely across the flat green sea of Missouri.

I flew one clod who turned out to be drunk; after we were airborne he made as though to climb out of the front cockpit, and generally proved himself a fool. I gave him a few hard turns to smash him down in the seat, all the time wishing that it would be legal to let the blockhead throw himself out of the airplane.

"You give me another passenger like that, Stu," I said after landing, "and I will part your hair with a crescent wrench."

"Sorry. Didn't know he was so bad."

The sun went down, but Spence kept hopping passengers. To each his own, I thought. The Parks and I quit as soon as we lost ground detail in the darkness.

It was full dark when at last he shut down his engine. In fourteen years with Pacific Southwest Airlines he was conditioned to haul every person he could possibly fly.

We collapsed on our sleeping bags and broke out the flashlight. "How'd we do, Stu?"

Stu heaped up the money. "We've got quite a bit. Twenty, thirty, thirty-five, forty-five . . ." It did look like it had been a good day. ". . . one fifty-three, fifty-four, fifty-five . . . one hundred and fifty-six dollars. That is . . . fifty-two passengers today."

"We broke it!" I said. "We broke our hundred-dollar day!"

"I tell you guys," Spence said. "This is not a bad way to make a living! Man, I wish I didn't have to get back so soon."

"We've got to get you some hayfield somewhere, Spence. Some little field for real barnstorming-type flying."

"There's not much time," he said. "Might have to wait till next year."

Stu's time was running out, too, and he talked with Spence about hitching a ride home.

I flew two leftover passengers the next morning, and we loaded our airplanes. Spence had one day left.

We took off west, and idled down the road, looking for a field-bordered town. It was as bad as ever. The fields were beautiful between the little villages. The hay was mowed and raked and baled away, and the land stretched long and clear into the wind.

But as soon as we approached a town, the telephone poles shot up like giant bamboo and the fields went short and rough and crosswind. We drifted down to look at a few borderline places, but nothing good came. We were not starving, and there was no need to work a difficult place.

Finally, over Lancaster, Missouri, we saw a field. It would be none too good—ridge-top land with steep hillsides to go tumbling down if we didn't roll straight out after landing—but it was long enough, and close to town.

Just after I pointed it out to Spence and Stu, I saw that the darn thing was an airport. No hangars, no gas pump, but the wheel-marks were there to give it away.

We were getting tired of wandering, so we landed. During the rollout I had doubts about carrying passengers out of there, even if it was an airport.

I watched the Travelair land. Smooth as a river, it flowed down the strip; the sight of an old pro at work, no matter how much Nelson protested his amateur status at barnstorming.

A low sign by a log in the grass said, "William E. Hall Memorial Airport."

"What do you think, Spence?" I said when he had shut down his engine.

"Looks OK. Fun comin' in. I went over town and revved the engine. I could see people down there, and they stopped, you know, and they were lookin' up."

"Well, we're close enough to town, but I don't quite dig the airport. It's a bit squirrelly for me, and if you lose the engine on takeoff you got no place to go without bending the airplane."

A car drove up and a man got out, carrying a movie camera. "Hi," he said, "mind if I take some pictures?"

"Go right ahead." The rest of our meeting was recorded in living color, to the whir of a spring-wound camera.

"I don't like it," I said. "We're not far south of Ottumwa, and that's home base for me. We need fuel anyway. Why don't we hop up there and get gas and oil and you can check the weather going west. Make a decision then."

"Let's do it."

We were airborne a few minutes later, heading north, and in half an hour we landed at Ottumwa, Iowa.

The weather growing in the west was not encouraging, and

Spence was worried. "They've got some pretty strong stuff coming down our way," he said. "High winds and low ceilings. I think I better hold the barnstorming till next year, Dick. If I get caught out by the weather I won't make my airline schedule. That wouldn't be too good. I better get out today and try to beat this stuff."

"Stu, you make up your mind?" I asked. "Last chance for a free ride home, probably."

"I guess I'd better go back with Spence," he said. "It's been a pretty good time . . . I'd be stretching it a little if I stayed. School starting before too long."

They packed up the Travelair at once; parachutes and oil and clothes bags and shaving kits. I cranked the engine alive and handed one of the *FLY $3* signs to Stu. "Souvenir, Mister MacPherson."

"You gonna autograph it for me?"

"If you want." I laid it out on the wing and wrote, SEE YOUR TOWN FROM THE AIR!, then signed it and handed it up to him as he made his place in the front cockpit.

I shook hands with Spence. "Glad you could make it. You're pretty nutty to come all the way across the country for two days' barnstorming."

"It was fun! We'll do it again next year, huh?"

I stepped up on the wingwalk and nodded once to the young jumper, wondering how to say goodbye. "Good times, Stu," I said at last. "Do what you want to do, remember."

"Bye." Way down in his eyes, the glimmer of a signal that he was learning, and for me not to worry.

The big biplane taxied out to the runway, pointed into the increasing wind and swept along up into the air. There were two quick waves from the cockpits and I waved back, thinking of myself through their eyes, a lone figure down on the ground, getting smaller and smaller and finally lost in distance. I stood there and watched the Travelair until the sound of it was gone, then until the sight of it disappeared in the west. And then there was nothing left in the sky. Stu, and Spence, too, had joined Paul. Gone, but not gone. Dead, but not dead at all.

I was surrounded by modern airplanes on the parking ramp, but for some reason as I walked back among them, I felt that it was they that were out of their time, and not I.

CHAPTER EIGHTEEN

THE AFTERNOON SKY WAS LOW GRAY, light rain whipped across the windscreen, and The Great American Flying Circus was down to one man, one biplane, alone in the air.

I had one tank of gasoline, and eleven cents cash in my pocket. If I wanted to eat again, I had to find somebody down there with three dollars and a burning wish to fly in the rain.

Prospects did not look good. Kirksville, Missouri, canceled itself in rows on rows of alfalfa bales in the hayfields and flocks of sullen cows in the pastures. And in Kirksville the rain poured solid down, intent on turning the city into a major inland sea; the windscreen changed into a sheet of water bolted to the airplane. It was not comfortable flying.

As we turned from Kirksville, spraying rain, I remembered a town on the way north that was worth a try. But again it was the wrong moment to strike. One good field, a block from town, was covered in hay bales. Another was surrounded by a fence. A third lay at the bottom of a square maelstrom of high-tension lines.

We circled and thought, the biplane and I, ignoring the grass airstrip and hangars a mile south. It would be a good town to work, but a mile away was too far. Nobody walks a mile in the rain to fly any airplane. At last, with the heavy Kirksville rains almost caught up with us again, we landed in the field with the fence, hoping there would be a gate. As the wheels touched, a fox leaped for cover in a neighboring stand of corn.

There was no break in the fence, but the two boys appeared, playing the part assigned them by destiny, rain or sun.

"Hey, where's the gate?"

"Isn't any gate. We climbed over. There's an airport just down the way, mister."

It was raining harder. "You boys know of any way a body could get in here, if I was to take 'em for an airplane ride?"

"Sure don't know. Climb the fence, I guess."

Another field crossed off the list. The airport, then. They might know there of some other place. Another two hours and it would be too dark to fly, with the rain and cloud hiding the sun. I chose the airport, because I didn't know where else to go.

Even that was a struggle. Along one side of the strip was a fence, along the other side a sea of corn. It was harder to land on that airport than on any hayfield we had worked, and I thought that even if this place was swarming with passengers I wouldn't fly one of them. It was all I could do to keep the biplane rolling straight between the solid obstacles, steering only by the high blur at each side of the cockpit and hoping that the path ahead was clear.

Waiting in the rain at the end of the strip were five metal hangars, a dripping windsock, and a pickup truck with an interested family within, watching. The man stepped shirtless from the driver's seat as I climbed from the cockpit, leaving the engine running.

"Want some gas?"

"No, thanks. Pretty good on gas. Looking for a place to fly."

I opened my road map and pointed to a town 20 miles south-west. "What do you know about Green City? Any place to land, there? Hayfield or pasture or somethin' like that?"

"Sure. They got a airport there. South of town, by the water reservoir. Whatcha doin'? Crop dustin'?"

"Carryin' passengers."

"Oh. Yeah, Green City might be nice. Probably a lot of people right here'd like to fly with you, though. You could stay right here, if you wanted."

"Bit too far from town," I said. "You have to be close to town. Nobody comes out if you're too far."

The rain slackened for a moment, and off to the southwest the sky didn't look quite as dark as it had an hour before. To fly again was to use gasoline that couldn't be replaced until we earned some money, yet if we stayed at the airport we would be jobless and hungry, both.

"Well, I'd better get goin'. Might as well push on off while there's light."

In a minute we were blurring between corn and fence, and then lifted above them and swung down into the south.

The hills in this part of Missouri roll on like green sea-billows, cresting in a fine spray of trees, sheltering roads and tiny villages in their troughs. It is not the easiest kind of country for navigators. There are none of the precise north-south section lines that lattice the states to the north. I sighted the nose a bit to the south of the lighter gray spot in the sky that was the setting sun.

Green City. What a name, what a poetic piece of imagery. I thought of tall wind-swayed elms, and streets of bright lawns, close-cut, and sidewalks in summer shade. I peered over the windscreen, looking for it. After a long moment, the town drifted in under the biplane's nose. There the reservoir, there the tall elms, there the water tower, all silver with the black letters GREEN CITY.

And there, good grief, the airport. A long strip along the crest of a ridge, narrower than the one I had just left. For a moment I wondered if the biplane would even fit in the width of it. At each edge, the ground dropped sharp and roughly away into tangled earth. The end was a row of barrels at the top of a cliff. Halfway down the strip was a metal building, almost overlapping the landing area. Green City was the most difficult airport to land upon that I had ever seen. I would not have picked that spot for a forced landing, even, if the engine stopped.

But there was a windsock, and a hangar. On the approach was a set of telephone wires, and as I flew a low pass down the field I saw that the last half of the strip was rolling, and tilted first to the left, then to the right. The narrow twisting runway was edged every fifty feet with tall white wooden markers. The owner must have figured that if you ran off the path you were going to hurt your airplane anyway, and a few wooden posts smashing into your wings wouldn't make that much difference. I saw that we'd have about eight feet clearance on each wingtip, and I swallowed.

We made one last pass over the field, and as we did, two motorcycles sped out the dirt road and braked hard at the edge of the grass to watch. As our wheels touched, I lost sight of the strip ahead, held my breath, and watched the white markers blur past the wingtips. I held the airplane as straight as I had ever held it and pressed down hard on the brake pedals. After an agonizing fifteen seconds, we had rolled to walking speed, and with much power and brake, the biplane turned very carefully in her tracks and taxied back to the road and the motorcyclists.

As I stepped out of the cockpit I wondered how much food and gasoline I could buy for eleven cents.

"You fellas feel like flyin'? Green City from the air; a real pretty place. Give you an extra long ride, since you came out to meet me so nice. Three dollars each, is all." I was aghast, listening to my own words. Carry passengers from this field? I am out of my mind!

But I had landed here once, and I could do it again. What was this airplane built for, but to fly passengers?

"Let's go, Billy!" one of the boys said. "I've never been up in one of these open jobs, and that's the kind Dad learned on. Can you carry us both?"

"Sure can," I said.

"Well, wait. I don't think we have the money."

They were leafing through their billfolds, picking sparse green bills. "Five-fifty is all we got between us. You fly us for that?"

"Well, since you came on out so quick . . . OK." I took the five dollar-bills and two pieces of silver and suddenly felt solvent again. Food! I would have steak tonight!

I emptied the cargo from the front seat and strapped my two passengers aboard, unconsciously pulling their safety belt a bit tighter than usual.

Settled down into my cockpit, I lined carefully on the bent strip of grass, and pushed the throttle forward. In spite of all the signs that I was going too far out on a shaky limb, I was glad to be aloft with my passengers. I had this moment gained title to that cash in my pocket, and after a few minutes buzzing around, I would have only to land and eat. I searched again for other places to come down, but there were none. Hills, money-crops, too short, too far from town. The motorcycles were still at the airport, anyway; we had to make one more landing on the high trapeze.

In ten minutes we circled the strip again, and in the dimming light it did not look any easier to land upon. The passengers were curious to see over the nose as we landed, and they blocked what little view I had in the moment I cut the throttle.

We hit the ground and bounced, and it felt as if we moved to the right. I thought of the embankment on the right side of the strip, and pushed left rudder. Too much. The biplane swerved left, and her left wheel went off the runway. By the time I hit right rudder, the left wing was flashing a foot above jumbled grassy hillocks and harsh earth there, streaking toward a wooden marker and that metal building. I slammed full right rudder and hit the throttle, rolling thirty miles per hour. The airplane jumped back onto the runway an instant before the building flashed by, and we swung hard to the right. I came back with full left rudder and full brakes. We stopped just at the edge of the embankment, and I went limp. So this is what barnstormers did when they were desperate for cash.

"Hey, that was great! Did you see 'em come runnin' out when we went over the house?"

My passengers couldn't have been nearly as happy as I was to be down again, and I gratefully took a ride to town on the back of a motorcycle.

The town square was a small Kahoka. There were picnic tables in the park, a Liberty Bell on a stand, a home plate and pitcher's mound, and a telephone booth with the glass broken out on the home-plate side. Square store fronts looked at the park from all four sides, and one of the squares was Lloyd's Café. Lloyd was sweeping out, and the place was empty.

"I could fix somethin' for you," he said, "but you probably wouldn't care much for my cookin'. Wife's out shoppin'."

The Town House Grill (Stop-N-Eat) was closed. Only Martha's was left, across the corner from Lloyd's. Martha's was not only open, but had two customers inside. I took a table and ordered my hamburgers and chocolate shakes, feeling rich. How money can change! On a good day, six dollars was nothing, a tiny droplet in the great bucket of prosperity. Today, my $5.50 was wealth, because it was more than I needed. Even after supper and corn chips and candy bars, I had four dollars clear.

Walking back to the biplane, I was an intruder in the town. Lights were coming on in the houses and voices drifted to the sidewalk. Now and then someone puttered in a dark flower garden, and looked up to watch me pass. The roofcrests of the houses carried strange ornaments, dragonlike, silhouettes of Viking ships, all cut from metal.

The reservoir was only a short walk from the biplane, and I turned aside. The ground was soft and hidden in deep grass. Flowers were tiny pure palettes strewn carelessly about. Reeds shuddered along the shore, more like arrows down from the sky than plants up from the water. Across the way a frog clacked like a Spanish castanet, and an invisible cow said, "mmMMMm," loud, out in the distance. The reservoir was a tiny Walden, with only the smallest ripples across its dark-mirror face.

I crunched back through the grass to the biplane and unrolled the sleeping bag. The moon went in and out of the clouds while the evening melted into night. I ate a lemon-drop, and listened to the sound of the engine still roaring in my ears. Solitude, I decided, is barnstorming all by yourself.

At nine a.m. on a day I didn't know, we circled Milan, Missouri, trailing sound and color, and landed in a hayfield a half-mile away. Before I had the sign on the gatepost, the first townsfolk arrived. Two pickup trucks clattered down onto the furrows and the drivers stepped out looking.

"Have a little motor trouble, did y'?" He was an old fellow, in coveralls.

"Aw, no," I said. "Flyin' around, givin' airplane rides."

"What d'y know. She's an old one, all right, too."

"Feel like a ride today? Nice and cool up there."

"Oh, no. Not me," he said. "I'm scared."

"Scared! This airplane been flyin' since 1929! Don't you think she might make one more flight without crashin' all to flinders? I don't believe you're scared."

"She'd go down sure enough if I got in there."

I pulled my sleeping bag from the front cockpit and turned to the other watcher.

"Ready to fly today? Three dollars, and Milan from the air. Pretty town it is."

"I'd go, if I could keep one foot on the ground."

"Can't see much from that height." It was clear that I wasn't going to be deluged with customers. My only hope had been that the biplane would be a strange enough thing in an airportless town to bring out the curious. Something had to happen soon. The fuel stick showed that we were down to 24 gallons of fuel. We'd need more gasoline before long, and we'd need passengers first, to pay for it. We had come from poor to rich to poor again.

A bright red late-model Ford sedan drove through the gate, purring in its mufflers. Instead of a license plate on its front bumper, it said CHEVY EATER. From the little crossed flags in chrome on the fender, I thought it might have some kind of huge engine under the hood.

The driver was an open-faced young man, a sort of enlightened hot-rodder, and he walked over to look in the cockpit.

"Feel like flyin' today?" I said.

"Me? Oh, no. I'm a coward."

"Hey, what is with all this coward stuff? Everybody in Milan scared of airplanes? I just better pack up and move out."

"No . . . there'll be lots of folks out to fly with y'. They just don't know you're here yet. You want to ride in town, get somethin' to eat?"

"No thanks. Might ride over to that place over there, though. What is it, a Buick place? Think they'd have a Coke machine?"

"Sure, they got one there," he said. "Come on, I'll give you a ride over. I'm not doin' anythin' anyway."

The pickup trucks had left and no one else appeared on the road. It seemed as good a time as any for breakfast.

The big engine was there in the Ford, and tires screeched all the way down the road.

"You flyin' that airplane came in a while ago?" the Buick dealer asked when I walked into his shop.

"Sure am."

"Not havin' any trouble, are you?"

"Nope. Just flyin' around givin' rides."

"Rides? How much do you get for a ride?"

"Three dollars. Trip over town. About ten minutes. You got a Coke machine?"

"Right over 'gainst the corner. Hey, Elmer! Stan! Go take an airplane ride with this guy. I'll pay your way."

I dropped a dime in the machine while the owner insisted that he was serious, and that his boys were to go out and fly.

Elmer put down his socket wrench at once. "Let's go." Stan wouldn't budge. "No, thanks," he said. "Don't quite feel like it today."

"You're scared, Stan," my Ford driver said. "You're scared to go up with him."

"I don't see *you* flyin', Ray Scott."

"I told him. I'm scared. Maybe I'll go up later."

"Well, I'm not scared of any old airplane," Elmer said.

I finished my Coke and we piled into the red Ford. "I was a special jumper in Korea," Elmer said as we drove. "Used to go up in a Gooney Bird and jump out from three thousand feet, with a ten-foot chute. Ten foot eight inches. I'm not scared of no airplane ride."

"A *ten-foot* chute?" I said. Elmer would have been hitting the ground at about forty miles an hour.

"Yeah. Ten foot eight inches. You know that I'm not afraid of no airplane ride."

The Ford stopped at the wing of the biplane and my passenger climbed aboard. In a minute we were airborne, engine and air thundering about us, the land piled in hills of crushed emerald below. We turned over town, trying to herd some passengers out to the hayfield. People on the ground stopped and looked up at us, and some boys on bicycles began wheeling out, and I had hope.

Elmer was not enjoying the flight. He braced himself hard against the side of the cockpit, and he didn't look down. Why, the man was frightened! There must be quite a story behind the guy, I thought. We glided down to land and he got out before the engine had windmilled to a stop. "See? Nothing about an airplane ride can scare me!"

Wow, I thought, and wondered about that story.

"Ready to go for a ride now, Ray?" he said.

"Maybe this afternoon. I'm scared."

"Ray, darn it," I said, "why is everybody in this town so scared of airplanes?"

"I don't know. Well, we had a couple pretty bad airplane crashes here this year, right around here. Guy got lost around Green City and went into a cloud and then crashed onto a hill. Then a little ways north a two-engine plane, brand new one, had the motors stop and hit a lot of trees and rocks. Killed everybody. People still worried, I guess. But you'll get some out after work, today."

So that was it. With airplanes falling like silly moths out of the air, no wonder the people were frightened.

When they left, in a screech of blue tire smoke, it was time for decision. I had $6.91 in my pocket, and 22 gallons of gasoline. If I waited there with no passengers, I'd be wasting time and getting hungrier. I couldn't spend money for lunch, or there would be nothing for gas. Later on, there might be passengers. And there might not. I wished Paul was there, or Stu or Dick or Spence, to be Leader for the Day, but I was stuck with Leader, and at last I decided to spend my money on gas, now. Maybe there would be a good town on the way north.

Centerville was 40 miles away, and there was an airport there. I loaded the front cockpit, started the engine with the crank, running back to the starter engage handle before the big whining wheel ground down, and took off north. It wasn't until we had been in the air for ten minutes that I thought $6.91 wasn't going to buy much aviation gasoline. Thirteen, fourteen gallons, maybe. I should have stayed to fly more passengers. But there was nothing to be done about it then, midway between Milan and Centerville. The best plan was just to pull the throttle back and use as little fuel as possible.

Car gas, I thought. The old engines were built for low-octane fuel. I knew antique-airplane pilots who used nothing but Regular auto gas in their engines. Someday I'll try car gas, when I don't have passengers to fly—see how it works.

Centerville swept serenely under the wing, and five minutes later we rolled to the 80-octane pump.

"What'll it be?" the attendant said. "Want some gas?"

"Take some 80-octane from you."

He pushed a lever that started the pump humming, and handed up the nozzle to where I stood in struts and wires over the gas tank. I rechecked my cash supply and said, "Tell me when I've got . . . six dollars and eighty-one cents' worth." I held back a dime for emergencies.

"Kind of a funny way to buy gas," he said.

"Yep." The nozzle poured fuel down into the black emptiness of the 50-gallon tank, and I was thankful for every second that it did. I had worked hard for that $6.81, and the fuel that it bought was precious stuff. Every drop of it. When the pump stopped, I held the nozzle there so that the last thin droplets fell down into the blackness. There was still a distressing amount of emptiness down the filler hole.

"Comes to sixteen gallons."

I handed down the hose and with it the money. Well, sixteen gallons was more than I thought I was going to get . . . now if I could go back to Milan at the lowest possible throttle setting, I might have a little more gas in the tank than I did when I left.

We chugged south with the engine turning 1575 revolutions per minute, nearly 200 rpm slower than low-cruise power. We crawled through the air, but the time that it took to get back to Milan was not so important as the amount of fuel we used. In 30 minutes we had covered 30 miles, and glided once again to land on the hay. No one waited.

Since I couldn't afford fuel for aerobatics, since Stu and his parachute were 1500 miles away, I was left with Method C. I unrolled the sleeping bag under the right wing, and resolved to employ C for one hour. If there were no passengers by then, I'd move on.

I studied the hay stubble a few inches away. It was a huge jungle, with all kinds of beasts roaming it. Here was a great crack in the earth, wide enough to keep an ant from crossing. Here was a young tree of a hay-stem growing new, a half-inch tall. I pulled it up and ate it for lunch. It was tender and tasty, and I looked for others. But that was it, the other hay was all old and tough.

A spider climbed a tall grassblade and threatened to jump down onto my sleeping bag and torment me. Easily met, that challenge. I uprooted the blade and moved the spider two feet south. I rolled over and looked up at the bottom of the wing for a while, and drummed my fingers on its tightness.

One-thirty. In half an hour I'd be on my way . . . the people here were just too frightened. That little town of Lemons, on the way to Centerville, might have some chances.

A pickup truck clattered down toward me. Like every pickup in every town, it had its owner's name painted on the door. *William Cowgill, Milan, Mo.* I read upside down, under the wing. A black pickup truck.

I got up and rolled my sleeping bag; it was time to leave.

An interested sharp mind peered at me from under a shock of white hair, through quick blue eyes.

"Howdy," I said. "Lookin' to fly at all today? Nice and cool up there."

"No thanks. How y' doin'?" Next to him sat a boy of twelve or so.

"Not too good. Not too many people feel like flyin', 'round here, I guess."

"Oh, I don't know. Think you'd probably get quite a few this evening."

"This is too far out," I said. "You got to be close to town, or nobody even sees you."

"You might have better luck over at my place," he said. "It's not too far out."

"Sure didn't see it from the air. Where is it?"

The man opened the door of the truck, took a wide board from the back and drew a map. "You know where the cheese factory is?"

"No."

"Lu-Juan's?"

"No. I know where the school is, with the race track."

"Well, you know the lake. The big lake, south of town?"

"Yeah. I know that."

"We're just across the street from that lake, on the south. Ridge land. There's some cows in the place now, but we want 'em out anyway and you can land there. Fact, I've been thinking of making an airport out of it. Milan needs an airport."

"Guess I could find that. Just across from the lake." I was sure that the pasture wouldn't work, but I had to be on my way anyway, and I might as well have a look at it.

"Right. I'm driving the truck, and Cully here's got the jeep at the corner. We'll go on over and meet you."

"OK. I'll look at it, anyway," I said, " 'f it don't work out, I'll be on my way."

"All right. Cully, come on." The boy was standing by the cockpit, looking at the instruments.

In five minutes, we were circling a strip of ridged pasture. A flock of cows clustered around the center, apparently eating the grass. We dropped down for a low pass, and the land looked smooth. The pasture was on the side of a long hill, and rose like a gentle roller-coaster to the crest. Just beyond the crest was a barbed-wire fence and a row of telephone poles and wires. If we rolled off the ridge-line, we'd be in trouble, but then if we did that it would be our own fault. Carefully used, this would be a good strip to work from. We could take off downhill and land uphill.

Best of all, there was a hamburger stand a hundred yards down the road. If I carried only one passenger, I could eat!

The cows galloped away after the first pass over their horns. There was one scrap of paper on the whole strip, a crushed newspaper just by a place where the ridge turned right. As soon as I saw that paper go by, I'd touch right rudder, just a little.

It was more difficult than it looked, and our first landing was not as smooth as I wanted it to be. But cars were already parking by the fence to watch the biplane fly, and passengers came out at once.

"How much do you want for a ride?"

"Three dollars. Nice and cool up there, too." Passengers before the sign went up, I thought. A good omen.

"OK. I'll fly with you."

Haha, I thought, lunch. I emptied the front cockpit again, feeling that I had spent the whole day loading and unloading that front seat, and strapped my passenger aboard. The view from the ridge-top was a pretty one, rolling hills away off to the horizon, the trees and houses of the town they called "*My*-l'n" resting easy on a soft rise of ground. Taking off downhill, the biplane leaped ahead, was airborne in seconds, and climbed quickly over the fields.

We circled town, the passenger looking down at the square and the county courthouse centered there, the pilot thinking that he just might have found a good place to barn-storm. A circle to the left, one to the right, a turn over a private lake and boat dock, a gliding spiral down over the pasture, with a gathering row of automobiles waiting, and our second landing on the ridge-top. It went smoothly. The place would work. Finding this field was finding a diamond hidden in a secret green jewel-box.

It was a different town, here. The people were much more interested in the airplane, and they wanted to fly.

"You might go out east, over the golf course," Bill Cowgill said as he arrived in the pickup, "get some folks out there, maybe." He was more interested in making the flying a success than anyone we had worked with. Probably because he wanted to see how the land worked as an airport.

"How are you fixed for gas, Bill?" I said. "There a filling station around, have a five-gallon can of gas, regular car gas?"

"Got some down at the house, if you want. Got plenty."

"Well, I might take you up on ten gallons, maybe."

Two more men stepped from the cars. "You giving rides?" they said.

"Sure thing."

"Well, let's go." We went.

Circling to land, I saw that the cars had parked exactly across the end of my strip. If we touched down too long, and rolled straight along the ridge-line, we'd run right into the middle of them all. I cut the throttle back and decided that if we were rolling too fast, I'd turn left, down the side of the ridge, up the side of the crest and then deliberately ground-loop right. If everything went well, I wouldn't even damage the airplane. Still, I didn't want to land long.

As a result of all this thinking, we dropped in to a hard landing, bounced up into the air again, and staggered along the ridge to a stop. It was a reminder that we didn't want to land too short, either.

From these first passengers I now had $9 in my pocket, and I left the airplane to her spectators for a while and walked across the street to the hamburger stand, Lu-Juan's. Ah, food! As the gasoline was precious to the biplane, so those two hot dogs and two milkshakes were precious to the pilot. I was happy just to sit there quietly and eat something more filling than hay.

The airplane now had a good crowd of spectators standing around her, and I began to worry about her fabric. I ordered an orange drink to go and then walked back to the airplane. There were passengers waiting to fly.

From time to time during lulls in the afternoon, Bill talked again about his field. "If you were going to make an airport out of this strip, what would you do to fix it up? For less than five hundred dollars, say."

"Wouldn't have to do much to it at all. Maybe fill that part right down at the end, though that would be a lot of fill. Wouldn't have to do that; all you'd have to do would be to mark out the levelest ground. That's the biggest problem, picking just where to touch down and roll out."

"You wouldn't say to level the place up?"

"I don't think so. Nothing better than takeoff downhill and land uphill. Just put down some lime or something like that, to mark where to land. Put in a gas pump later, if you wanted. With the lake there and the place to eat, this would be a nice little airstrip."

"How wide would you think it might be?"

"Oh, maybe from about here . . . over to about . . . here, would be wide enough. Be plenty wide."

He took a double-bit axe from the bed of the pickup and chopped a mark into the earth at each edge of the landing area.

"I'll just mark this off here and maybe some day we'll have something going."

As it happened to the first barnstormers, it happened to me. An axe marks the place where the first airplane lands, and someday in the future there are many airplanes landing. I didn't think till later that if this field were turned into an airstrip, there would be one less pasture in the world for barnstormers to fly from.

"I'll fly with you if you promise to fly real smooth . . ."

It was my red-Ford-driver and self-styled coward, Ray.

"You want to go up in that dangerous thing," I said, "that dangerous old airplane?"

"Only if you promise not to turn her over."

I had to smile, for despite all his words of fear, the man wasn't afraid at all; he rode the airplane like a veteran, the circle over the golf course, the two circles of town, the steep spiral over the strip, looking down, looking down, like it was all a dream of flying.

"That was really fun," he said, and went back to his car, happy.

"Free ride for the owner, Bill," I said to the elder Cowgill, "Let's go."

"I think Cully wants to ride more than I do."

Cully did, and pulled his own leather flying helmet from the jeep as he ran for the airplane. "Dad got it for me at the war surplus," he explained, climbing by himself into the front seat. He liked his ride before we ever got off the ground.

With my debts paid, and the last ride flown, I poured two five-gallon cans of Regular gas into the tank. Enough to fly alone, and to check the effect of car-gas on the engine. It worked just as smoothly as aviation fuel, if not a tiny bit smoother.

So, by sundown, I had flown twenty passengers and had $49 in my pocket after food and fuel. A good feeling from the hayfield noon, with a dime to my name.

I knew now, without question, that the land of yesterday does exist, that there is a place of escape, that a man can survive alone with his airplane, if only he has a wish to do so. Milan had been good to me, and I was happy. But tomorrow it would be time to move on.

❦ CHAPTER NINETEEN ❦

THE DAYS FOLDED ONE INTO ANOTHER, and into events of August and September. County fairs, with special brushed cows and combed sheep waiting for judgment, dining only on the cleanest of polished straw.

Coins raining down on glassware with the sound of wind chimes in the night, above the song of the barker: "Nickel in the crystal glass, folks, and it's yours to take home. Toss a nickel and win a glass . . ."

Quiet streets, old towns; where the Vogue Theater had been turned into a machine shop, and finally closed.

People with memories of old airplanes flying, and of droughts and floods, the good and bad of decades.

Foot-tall jars of Mrs. Flick's Oatmeal Cookies, three for five cents.

Pioneer-dressed women in small-town celebration, and square dances in the streets.

Music amplified and echoing through the starlight, rippling across the still wings of a biplane and through the silken hammock of a barnstormer listening, watching the galaxy.

A great burly grizzled mountain of a man, Claude Shepherd, tending his monster-iron Case Steam Tractor, built

1909. Twenty tons of metal, barrels of water, bunkers of coal, giant huge bull gears driving wheels seven feet tall. "I got to love steam power from the time I was a little tad, on my grandfather's knee. Smoothest power in the world, steam. When I was five, I could set the valves . . . never got over it, never got over lovin' steam."

Passengers, passengers, men and women and children rising up to see the sky, to look down on the water towers of towns everywhere Midwest. Every takeoff different, every landing different, every person in the cockpit ahead a different person, guided into gentle adventure. Nothing happened by chance, nothing by luck.

Sunrise into sunset into sunrise. Wild clear air, rain and wind and storm and fog and lightning and wild clear air again.

Sun fresh and cool and yellow like I'd never seen. Grass so green it sparkled under the wheels. Sky blue and pure like skies always used to be, and clouds whiter than Christmas in the air.

And most of all, freedom.

✠ CHAPTER TWENTY ✠

THEN CAME A DAY when we took off, the biplane and I, into Iowa.

Chugging north, looking down. One town had a good hayfield, and we circled and landed. But the margin wasn't there. If the engine stopped on takeoff there was only rough ground ahead. There are those who say that the chances of engine failure on takeoff are so remote that they aren't worth worrying about, but those people do not fly old airplanes.

We took off again and turned farther north, into the cold air of autumn. The towns here were islands of trees, isolated by seas of cornfields ready for harvest. The corn grew right close in to town, and there weren't many possible places to work. But I wasn't worried. The question of survival had long since been answered. Some good place always showed up by sundown.

I had just discarded another small town when the engine choked, one time, and a puff of white smoke whipped back in the windstream. I sat up straight in the seat, tense as iron.

The smoke was not good. The Wright never acted strangely unless it was trying to tell me that something was wrong. What was it trying to say? Smoke . . . smoke, I thought. What could make a puff of white smoke? The engine was running smoothly again. Or was it? Listening very carefully, I thought that it was running the slightest bit roughly. And I could smell the exhaust more than I usually could. But all the instruments were pointing in their proper places: oil pressure, oil temperature, tachometer . . . just as they should have been.

I pushed the throttle forward and we climbed. Just in case something was wrong, I wanted more altitude for gliding if everything went to pieces and we had to land in the gentle hills below.

We leveled at 2500 feet in icy air. Summer was over.

Was there a fire under the cowl? I looked over the side of the cockpit, out into the wind, but there was no sign of fire forward.

There was something wrong with the engine. There! It was running rough, now. If the engine would stop, that would be one thing, cause for definite action. But this roughness, and the smell of the exhaust, and that puff of smoke. It all meant something, but it was hard to tell what . . .

At that instant, a great burst of white smoke flew back from the engine, a solid river dragging back in a dense trail behind. I looked over the right side of the cockpit and saw nothing but smoke, as if we had been shot down, in real combat.

Oil sprayed windscreen and goggles. We are in trouble, airplane.

I thought again that we were on fire, which would not be good in a wood-and-fabric airplane, half a mile in the air. I shut down the engine and turned off the fuel, but still the smoke poured overboard, a long helpless streak across the sky. Great Scott. We are on fire.

I kicked the biplane hard up on her wing, slammed full rudder, and we slipped wildly sideways toward the ground.

There was an open field there, with a hill, and if we played it just right . . .

The smoke came thinner and finally stopped, and the only sound was the quiet whistle of the wind through the wires and the faint clanking of the propeller as it fanned around.

There was a tractor working the other side of the sloping field, mowing hay. I couldn't tell whether he saw us or not, and at the moment, I didn't care.

Level out, cross the fence, slip off a little speed, catch the hill on the rising side . . .

We touched, and I forced the control stick hard back, digging the tailskid deep into the ground. We rolled across the peak of the hill, rumbling, clattering, slowed, and stopped.

I sat in the cockpit for a moment, thankful that the airplane had been under control every second. Perhaps there was only something minor wrong. A valve, maybe, or a hole in a piston, pumping oil into a cylinder.

I got out of the cockpit and walked to the engine. There was oil streaming from every exhaust port, and when I moved the propeller, oil gurgled inside. This was nothing simple.

I unbolted the carburetor and remembered one of Pop Reid's adventures. "Supercharger oil seal," he had said, years ago. "She blew three gallons of oil in two minutes flat. Had to tear down the whole engine."

In a few minutes the answer was clear. A bearing in the center of the engine had come to pieces, and oil poured with the fuel into all cylinders. That's where we got the smoke, and the oil on my goggles.

The Whirlwind, at the end of summer, was finished.

I accepted a ride from the farmer and rode into Laurel, Iowa, on his tractor. A call to Dick Willetts, and he was on his way with the Cub. Thank God, again, for friends.

I went back to the biplane and covered her for the nights ahead. There was no spare engine. I could come here with a truck and take this engine home for rebuild, or I could take the whole airplane home on a trailer. Either way, it would be a while before she flew again.

The little yellow Cub was a beautiful sight in the sky, and Dick set her down on the hilltop lightly as a feather in a pillow factory. We would leave, and the Parks would stay in her field. I climbed into the back seat of the Cub, and we lifted over the hay and homeward. The plane looked lost and lonely as she dwindled in distance.

All the hour's flight, I wondered about the meaning of the engine failure, why it stopped the way it did and where it did and when it did. There is no such thing as bad luck. There's a reason and a lesson behind everything. Still, the lesson may not always be simple to see, and by the time we landed at Ottumwa, I hadn't seen it. I had only one question about the engine failure: Why?

The only thing to do was to bring the biplane home. The first windstorm could hurt her, the first hailstorm destroy her. She did not belong out in the weather with winter rolling down upon us.

I borrowed a pickup truck and a long flatbed trailer from Merlyn Winn, the man who sold Cessna airplanes at Ottumwa airport, and three of us traveled the 80 miles north; a young college friend named Mike Cloyd, Bette and I. Somehow we had to find a way to take the airplane apart and lash it onto that trailer, and to do it in the five hours left before dark. We wasted no time at the job.

"She looks kind of sad, don't she?" Mike said, when the wings lay yellow and frail on the hay.

"Yeah." I agreed only because I didn't feel like talking. The machine didn't look sad to me. It looked like a bunch of mechanical parts disconnected across the ground. The thing was no longer alive, was no longer a she, no longer a personality. There was no chance of it flying now, and the only life it knew was when it was flying, or able to fly. Now it was wood and steel and doped cloth. A pile of parts to load on a trailer and take home.

At last it was done and it was just a matter of sitting in the cab and pointing the truck down the road until we reached home. I still couldn't understand why this was all happening, what important thing I would have missed if the engine had not failed.

We turned onto Interstate 80, all modern and highspeed pavement. "Mike, keep an eye on the trailer, will you, see if anything's gonna fall off, now and then?"

"Looks all right," he said.

We accelerated up to 40 miles an hour, glad to be on the fast road home. It would be good to get this game over with.

At 41 miles an hour, very slightly, the trailer began fish-tailing. I looked in the rear-view mirror and touched the brake. "Hang on," I said, and wondered why I would say that.

The trailer took ten seconds to play its part. From a gentle fishtail, it swerved harder left and right, and then it lashed sudden and wild from one side to another behind us, a whale shaking a hook from its jaw. Tires screamed again and again, and the truck was slammed heavily to the left. We were out of control.

The three of us were interested bystanders, sitting together in the cab of the truck, unable to steer or stop. We slid side-ways, then backward, and I looked out the left window to see the trailer smashed against the side of the truck, glued there, while we went off the road. I could have reached out and touched the big red fuselage for a while, but then we slid into the grass valley between the two highways of the Interstate.

The dead body of the airplane lurched up on one wheel, teetered there a second in slow motion and then slowly went crashing upside-down into the ditch. I sat idly and watched the centersection and its struts crush down in no hurry at all, bending, tearing, splintering away under the thousand-pound fuselage. It was all very quiet. How like a paper bag, I thought, the way it folds up.

We came to a stop, all in a neat row: truck, trailer, fuselage; like sea-creatures caught and laid side by side in the grass.

"Everybody OK?" Everybody was fine.

"I can't open the door on this side, Mike, trailer's jamming it. Let's get out on your side."

I was disgusted. The lesson escaped me entirely. If there is nothing by chance, just what in God's name was this all supposed to mean?

The fuselage that we had just barely managed to strain onto the trailer through brute force was now upside down, wheels in the air. Gasoline and oil poured from the tanks. The lower wings were trapped between the trailer and the airplane body, holes torn through them. One engine rocker-box was pounded flat, where it had struck concrete. We might as well set the thing on fire, I thought, and drive home alone. It's dead, it's dead, it's dead.

"The hitch busted," Mike said. "Look, it tore right out of the bumper, tore the metal right out."

It was so. Our trailer hitch was still firmly coupled and lashed, but it had been ripped bodily from the heavy steel of the bumper. It would have taken at least five tons on the hitch to shear it free, and the complete load on the trailer was a little over a tenth of that.

What were the chances of this happening, on the one time I had ever put the biplane on a flatbed trailer, on the only time she had not been able to fly herself out of a field, with a truck and trailer that had been designed for hauling airplanes? A million to one.

Cars and trucks stopped along the roadside, to help and to watch.

A truck driver brought a heavy jack, and we lifted the pickup free of the trailer, undamaged, and drove it up to the edge of the highway. By now it was full dark, and we worked in the beams of headlights; it all felt like a Dante nightmare.

With ten men, and with a heavy rope tied from truck to fuselage, we finally dragged what was left of the biplane back onto its wheels, and forced it again onto the trailer. I wondered how we were going to tow a trailer without a hitch, or even move the trailer out of the low grass valley.

A great boxy truck stopped by the plane, and the driver got down. "Can I help you?" he said.

"Kinda doubt it; can't do too much more, I guess. Thanks."

"What happened?"

"Hitch broke off."

The man walked to look at the broken metal. "Hey, look," he said. "I have a hitch on my truck, and I don't have to be in Chicago for another couple days. Maybe I can tow you somewhere. I'm kind of interested in airplanes . . . airline pilot out of Chicago. Don Kyte's the name. Coming home from California. I'd be glad to help you, if I could."

About that time I came awake to what was happening. Again . . . what are the chances of this guy coming along this road in this month in this week in this day in this hour in this minute when I have no possible way to tow that trailer, and him coming along not only in a truck, not only in an empty truck, but in an empty truck with a trailer hitch on it, and he not only happens to like airplanes but he is an airline pilot and he has days to spare? What are the chances of a lucky coincidence like that?

Don Kyte backed his truck down into the valley, pulled the trailer straight, then hitched up to it and pulled it onto the road.

The police arrived, then, and an ambulance, red lights flashing in the dark. "Anybody hurt?" the officer said.

"Nope. Everybody's fine."

He ran back to his patrol-car radio to report this, and then came slowly out to see the trailered airplane. "We heard there was an airplane crash on the Interstate," he said.

"Sort of, yeah." I explained what had happened.

"Any cars damaged?" He began to write on a clipboard.

"No."

He held his pencil, and thought. "No cars damaged, nobody hurt. This isn't even an accident!"

"No, sir, it isn't. We're all ready to move on, now."

We unhitched the trailer by the Ottumwa hangar at midnight, and Don came to stay the night with us. We found that we had mutual friends from one coast to another, and it was past two when we finally folded the couch down into a bed for him and let him alone to sleep.

The next day I went to the airport and unloaded airplane-parts, stacking them in the back of the hangar.

Merlyn Winn walked to meet me, his footsteps echoing in the giant place.

"Dick, I don't know what to say. That hitch was welded into bad iron there, and it just picked this time to go. Gosh, I'm sorry about what happened."

"It's not all so bad, Merlyn. Centersection and struts, biggest part. Engine had to be overhauled, anyway. Some work on the wings. Be a good winter job."

"Nice thing about old airplanes," he said. "You just can't kill 'em dead. Shame it had to happen, though."

A shame it had to happen. Merlyn left, and in a moment I walked out from the hangar into the sunlight. It never would have happened at all if we had stayed home, if the biplane and I had only flown on Sunday afternoons, around the airport. I'd have no smashed airplane, then, no parts awaiting rebuild in the hangar. There would have been no crash at Prairie du Chien, picking up a handkerchief with a wingtip. No crash at Palmyra, as Paul met his challenge. No crash on Interstate 80, when a trailer hitch strangely failed.

There would have been no Stu plummeting down through the air, or puzzling us with his silent thoughts, or having the most continuous fun of his life. No mouse attacking my cheese. No passengers turning in the air for the first time, no "That's great!" no *"WONDERFUL!"* no immortality in Midwest family albums. No crumpled money-piles, no proof a gypsy pilot can survive, if he wishes, today.

No Claude Shepherd, by his giant hissing monster engine, talking the wonders of steam. No county fairs, no mosquito-hum at midnight, no honey-clover for breakfast, no formation flying in the sunset or sorrow of a lone airplane disappearing in the west. No freedom tasted, none of these strange affairs I called guidance to whisper that man is not a creature of chance, pointed into oblivion.

A shame? Which would I rather have, the wreck in the hangar or a polished piece of a biplane that flew only on calm Sunday afternoons?

I walked across the concrete ramp in the sun, and for a moment I was in the biplane again and we were flying together beside the Luscombe and the Travelair, up in the wind, out over those green fields and towns of another time. I still didn't know the why of the wreck, but some day I would.

What mattered, I thought, was that the color and the time still waited for me, as they always had, just across the horizon of a special free enchanted land called America.

⚘ EPILOGUE ⚘

IT DIDN'T take a winter to rebuild the biplane, it took two years.

Two years of saving dollars and working on the wreck—lifting away the smashed wood and fabric, the broken struts, the remains of the engine. In that time I finished and covered a new centersection for the top wing, replaced a dozen splintered sections in the body and wings of the plane, stood guard with water while torches replaced bent fittings with hot new steel, while new struts were formed from streamlined tubing.

Bit by bit as the months turned past. Fuel tank repaired—month, month—windscreen replaced—month, month—coaming formed from wrinkled metal back into a smooth curve, and painted.

In that time one part of my being was locked there in pieces and bolts across the hangar floor, no longer free, asking, over and again, "Why?" I was glad to pay the price for the discovery of my country, yet it seemed so unnecessary, and that part of me in the hangar was a heavy sad part indeed.

Friends. What a pure and beautiful word. Dick McWhorter, in Prosser, Washington: "I still have a Whirlwind engine down in the hangar. It hasn't run since 1946, and you'd better check it, but it looks good. I'll hold it for you . . ."

John Howard, in Udall, Kansas: "Sure, I'd be glad to look at the engine for you. And say, I have some wing bolts . . ."

Pop Reid, in San Jose, California: "Oh, don't worry, kiddo. We have a collector ring for that engine, and all the connections—never been used. You might as well have it, it's just sitting around out here . . ."

Tom Hoselton, in Albia, Iowa: "I have more work than I know what to do with, but this is special. I'll have the fittings welded up for you in a week . . ."

Very slowly, years passing while I struggled to earn a living with a bargain-basement typewriter, the biplane changed in the square cocoon of its hangar.

Fuselage finished. Wings attached and rigged. Tail on. Engine mounted. New cowling.

And then the day came that the old propeller on the new engine jerked around in a blurred silver streak, and very suddenly the biplane, two years dead, was alive again, bouncing hard echoes off the hangar doors. Up ahead in the roar and the wind, the black rocker-arms clicked up and down, spraying new grease back from their uncovered boxes.

So long dead, and I was alive. So long chained, and I was free.

At last, the answer why. The lesson that had been so hard to find, so difficult to learn, came quick and clear and simple. The reason for problems is to overcome them. Why, that's the very nature of man, I thought, to press past limits, to prove his freedom. It isn't the challenge that faces us, that determines who we are and what we are becoming, but the way we meet the challenge, whether we toss a match at the wreck or work our way through it, step by step, to freedom.

And behind it, I thought, lifting the biplane up once again

into the sky, lies not blind chance but a principle that works to help us understand, a thousand "coincidences" and friends come to show us the way when the problems seem too hard to solve alone.

True for me, true for my country America.

We turned gently about a cloud, and flashed sunlight, a mile in the air, setting course for the towns of Nebraska.

Problems for overcoming. Freedom for proving. And, as long as we believe in our dream, nothing by chance.